Carole Achterhof

NEVER TRUST A SIZE THREE

Written and Illustrated By

CAROLE ACHTERHOF

Cover design by **JENNIFER FISHER**

Dedicated to Roger,
my best friend and husband,
who laughs the loudest.

Library of Congress Catalog Card Number: 90-92938
ISBN   0-9625940-0-8
First printing

Printed and manufactured in the United States
by Crescent Publishing, Inc., Hills, Minnesota 56138

Table of Contents

Never Trust a Size Three 5
Running 7
Memory Loss 9
The Bifocals 11
The Midlife Haircut 13
The Tanning Booth 15
My Dreams of Becoming a Lady 17
Dressed to Kill 19
The Bathing Suit Dilemma 21
I'm Short for my Weight 23
Talking Bathroom Scales 25
Great Expectations 27
Them 29
I Sing the Praises of Shoulder Pads 31
The Rummage Sale 33
Numbers 35
Who's the Boss? 37
The Pantyhose Problem 39
The VCR 41
The Frump 43
Ma'am? No Thanks! 45
The Plumber 47
The Scorch Factor 49
The Exercise Bike 51
Exercise 53
Halloween Candy 55
The Sweat Pants 57
The Diet 59
A Gift of Chocolates 61
Sweet Revenge 63
Life in the Slow Lane 65
Allowances 67
It's a Boy! It's a Girl! 69
Answering Machines 71
The Basement 73
Refrigerator Cultures 75
The Battle of the Thermostat 77
The Egg-splosion 79
Festival Hits the Mark 81
Golf 83
Putting the Byte into Computers 85
Moby Perch 87
The Sunglasses 89
SAD 91
The Septic Tank 93

Remote Control Blues 95
Blood Tests are in Vein 97
Pets are Forever 99
The Russians and the Checks 101
Chocolate is Good for your Teeth 103
The Tag Inspector 105
It's the Tooth 107
Flannel Nighties 109
The Dangers of Going Strapless 111
The Christmas Tree 113
Modern Music 115
Throwing in the Towel 117
Car Wash Blues 119
Clothes Encounters 121
Drive-up Deliveries 123
Cotton Makes a Comeback 125
Wedding Dresses 127
My Son, the Dustball 129
Daytime Soaps 131
Newspaper Models 133
The Dorm Bill 135
Credit Cards 137
The Garbage Can 139
The Chauffeur 141
The Nerd 143
Raking Leaves 145
The Toad 147
Storm Windows 149
Cow Boots 151
Water Rationing 153
Designer Sunglasses 155
Long Hair 157
All about Pi 159
Holstein Heaven 161
Oatmeal Cologne 163
The Miraculous Power Outage 165
The Dustballs 167
Today's Pet is Tomorrow's Pork Chop 169
High Tech Garbage 171
The Appraisal 173
Homecoming 175
Parental Pride 177
The Visit 179
Chocolate for Cows 181
About the Author 183

Never Trust a Size Three

My adult life has been divided into very distinct parts: a time when I wished to look pregnant and a time when I didn't.

For almost a decade nothing seemed to please me more than to let the world know that I was pregnant. The rabbits had barely cooled down before I was traipsing around in billowy blouses and tent-like dresses. At that time of svelte fashion styles, it was much easier to identify a pregnant woman in public.

It's almost embarrassing to admit this, but during that time of my life, I cared to think about very little other than babies, preparing layettes and the current prices of canned baby food. I was preoccupied with the idea of giving birth and could talk non-stop about the subject, much to the chagrin of those near and dear to me.

Times have changed. As our daughters have grown older, my fetish about babies has changed into concerns about curfews, college choices and how to afford their designer jeans.

I rarely go clothes shopping, but this week I found myself within charging distance of one of my favorite clothing stores.

Instead of finding a dress which would make me look slim, trim and at least 30 pounds lighter, I was confronted with countless racks of what appeared to be maternity dresses. Dresses with enough shoulder padding to make any woman look like Alex Karras. There were dresses roomy enough to accommodate not only one person but an entire family.

A sales clerk, who had a soft Southern drawl and appeared to be terminally anorexic, assured me that the dresses looked much nicer on a person than on a hanger.

Although I normally shrug off any advice from a woman who wears a size three, I trudged off to the dressing room with several voluminous creations thrown over my shoulder.

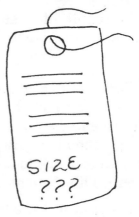

The next few minutes in front of the dressing room mirror were excruciatingly painful. As I struggled from one dress to another, I watched as my body was transformed from what appeared to be a sack of potatoes to a poor impression of Tugboat Annie to an entire flower show. In my case, the dresses looked much better on the hangers.

Undaunted, I returned the dresses and continued browsing through the store. Finally I came upon a collection of slenderizing styles. I knew that with one of these dresses, I would look like Minnesota's answer to Raquel Welch.

"Oh, no, honey", cooed Size Three. "These just won't do!" I was surprised that the sales clerk had had the physical stamina to follow me as I meandered through the aisles. I was even more surprised when she pointed out the sign above the display with her long, skeletal fingers: "Maternity Dresses". I quickly made my exit.

Running

Let's be perfectly honest. I don't do windows and I don't run.

A survey recently released by the *Los Angeles Daily News* revealed that 70 percent of Americans own running shoes but don't run. It's somehow reassuring to know that I have company.

Over the years I have accumulated a colorful assortment of running shoes. Unlike my car tires, they will never have to be retreaded.

I tried running in 1975. It was part of an intensive physical conditioning program that lasted for the better part of a day, and it marked perhaps one of the shortest running careers in history.

One day I decided to take a walk from our farm house to the highway, a reasonable round-trip distance of one and one-half miles. With unquenchable enthusiasm, which had only been reserved previously for desserts, I decided to record my walking time on a stopwatch.

Walking was a piece of cake. I duly recorded my walking time (30 minutes) on a chart which only took me a few minutes and four cookies to design. In a sugar-induced euphoria, I decided to run the same distance the next day, fully expecting to cut the total time by at least one-half.

Although I hadn't run for over 30 years, I expected that it was much like riding a bike. Once you learn, you never forget.

It was a sunny, crisp autumn afternoon when I set out for the big run the next day. As I started down the driveway, with running shoes on my feet and hope in my heart, I was running at a feverish pace. Hey, this was easy!

I continued running, and I could feel my pulse beating like a rhythmic drum and my muscles felt as though they had been done up in square knots. It was disconcerting, at this point, to discover that I had only reached the mailbox at the end of the driveway.

Once my nimble feet touched the gravel road, a steady running pattern began to assert itself. A run-walk pattern slowly became a run-stop-and-grab-your-side approach to running. By the time I reached the highway, I was giving serious thought to accepting the first ride that came along. I could no longer breathe and there was the distinct possibility that all oxygen to my brain would soon be cut off.

The trip home was equally unproductive. On at least three occasions, I sat down on the side of the road and contemplated my shoelaces and whether living 10 extra years was worth the pain.

By the time I reached the kitchen door, my entire body was numbed with exhaustion. I watched dully as my feet staggered into the kitchen on their own accord. It was the closest I have ever come to having an out-of-the-body experience.

In what appeared to be my final act as an earthly mortal, I glanced at the stopwatch. In no uncertain terms, the clock face read 48 minutes. To this day, I have never trusted another stopwatch.

They just don't make them like they used to.

Memory Loss

Losing my memory was a gradual process. Its onset occurred several years ago when I began forgetting the names of my children. Since my mother used to do the same thing, it must have some sort of genetic link. Until I was 10 years old, I couldn't be sure my name was Carole, David, Linda, Kathy or Charlie.

Before long I found myself doing the same thing. Whenever I wanted the attention of one of the girls, I would rattle off a list of all of their names. By the time all of the called names had rushed to my side, I usually forgot what I had wanted in the first place. It might have been easier to give the girls numbers rather than names.

As the years rolled by, my memory became progressively worse. More often than not, I have gone down to the basement to retrieve something only to discover that I have forgotten what it was by the time I reach the bottom stairstep.

Whenever I visit a large shopping mall, I invariably forget where I parked the car. At one large mall in Minneapolis, the parking areas are identified by pictures and names of animals. On one of my visits there, I spent a considerable amount of time in the Giraffe area searching for my car which had been parked by the Elephant sign.

My lapses of memory also extend to my workplace. My students are understandably miffed when I call them by their brothers' and sisters' names.

Recently I went grocery shopping and until I reached the checkout counter, my memory had served me fairly well. I had remembered by checkbook, my shopping list and where I had parked the car.

As I waited for the woman ahead of me to complete her purchases, I was feeling fairly confident. After she had handed over her check to the cashier, the woman began walking out of the store without her small bag of groceries.

"Maam! Maam!" shouted the checkout boy when she reached the door. "You've forgotten your groceries!" All heads turned to watch the woman, who was obviously embarrassed. For one brief moment, the store was awkwardly silent as we watched the woman mumble something to the checkout boy and then make a speedy exit through the automatic door.

In spite of my faulty memory, it was somehow consoling to realize that at least one person in the world had a worse memory than I had. I felt slightly smug knowing that I at least had never forgotten my groceries.

As I paid for my own small bag of groceries and talked about the weather with the man next in line, I made a small mental note that I would never do anything as embarrassing as leaving behind my groceries in the checkout lane.

After saying goodbye to the cashier and the man behind me, I left the store and was opening the car door when an all too familiar voice stopped me stone-cold in my tracks. At least twenty faces in the busy parking lot turned in my direction.

"Maam! Maam! shouted the carryout boy. "You've forgotten your groceries!"

Once more, there was a moment of awkward silence.

The Bifocals

Like Peter Pan, I never intended to grow older. I always figured that I would somehow beat the system and never have gray hair, age spots or bifocals.

Never has arrived. This past week I received my first pair of bifocals and I didn't realize that looking at things could be so complicated.

For the first few days, I spent most of my time trying to decide whether I should be viewing the world through the top or bottom halves of my new glasses.

It's somehow reassuring to know that other people have had to endure the adjustments, since Ben Franklin first invented bifocals back in 1785.

It was also comforting to read that a standard set of eyeglasses in 1785 cost $100, the equivalent of 15 months' pay in Washington's army.

There are few things for sale in this country with the same price tags they carried over 200 years ago.

Actually, people should be paid to wear bifocals. My first experience with the complex lenses began with an ominous work of advice from the optometric assistant.

"Don't look down when you walk home," she warned.

Not being a person who readily accepts the advice of other people, I looked down several times. There were street curbs the height of track hurdles and cracks in the sidewalks at least a foot wide.

I staggered the two blocks home like a sailor unaccustomed to walking on land.

Bifocals operate on a very simple principle. If you want to see far away, you look through the tops of the lenses. If you want to see something close up, you look through the bottoms.

It was easy to forget the principle. For the rest of the week, every household task seemed like another step into the Twilight Zone. I peeled carrots over three feet long, and I swatted flies larger than your average Thanksgiving turkey.

Even the simple act of applying lipstick took on new dimensions. My first attempt, while wearing bifocals, nearly resulted in a streak of bright red from ear to ear.

Fortunately, the period of adjustment passes, and wearing the bifocals now seems very natural, like sleeping on a bed of nails or walking barefoot over hot coals.

I realize that things could be worse. At least I still have my own teeth.

Although I may not have the same gleam in my eyes, the sun does reflect quite nicely off my bifocals.

The Midlife Haircut

It was a crazy, impulsive thing to do. If not giving into one's impulses is a sign of maturity, I must be about 12 years old.

For years, I have kept most of those wild impulses in check. On more than one occasion I have been sorely tempted to bite into a lipstick while I've applied it to my lips. When I see men with substantial beer bellies, wearing blue jeans low on their hips, heldup with nothing more than a hope and a prayer, I have thought about giving one of their back belt loops a little tug. I have come dangerously close to removing the tags which say "Do not remove under penalty of law" from our mattresses.

Through all of these temptations and others, I have remained a pillar of strength. One of the biggest reasons I have been able to refrain from doing those things is the haunting fear that my husband and children would change their names and leave home.

Today was different. I went to a beauty shop, ostensibly to get a trim. If I would have stuck with the idea of getting a little off the top and little off the sides, I wouldn't look like a Fuller brush gone amuck tonight.

As the plastic cape was draped around my shoulders and the woman asked me how I would like my hair cut, I suddenly found myself in one of those unpredictable mid-life crises. My hair has been cut the same way for years, and I began thinking about how I would probably be getting the same style two decades later.

"Give me a brush cut," a voice which wasn't mine

said. Not only are impulses fanciful, but they can also do perfect voice imitations.

"Are you sure? the woman asked.

"Of course, I'm sure," Impulse answered. I didn't say anything for fear of interrupting.

She pruned away and she hacked away. Sooner than I had thought possible, I had been shorn, glazed and moussed. If crazed porcupines are a wonder, I was a wonder to behold.

Since I left the shop, I have looked at my reflection in windows and mirrors at least a dozen times. I can't figure whether the new look is avant-garde or if it resembles an escapee from an asylum in one of those old Boris Karloff movies. After one look at me, mothers remind their small children not to stick their fingers in light sockets.

In all probability my hair will grow out. If worse comes to worse, I can always spray paint it green and stand in for our usual Christmas tree.

Whatever the outcome, my new look certainly makes a statement. To some people it might be saying, "How chic!" or "How daring!" I only hope that it's not proclaiming to all the world, "Look out, this mid-life crisis is a real doozy!"

The Tanning Booth

I succumbed recently to the slick pitches of the tanning bed ads. After all, who in their right mind wouldn't trade a funereal pallor for what the ads describe as a "savage, tropical tan"?

The ads had photographs of willowy, long-legged blondes with skin the color of butterscotch pudding. Before you could say "Am I peeling?", I had signed up for 10 sessions at the local swimming pool complex.

In order to pay for my tanning sessions, it was necessary to make some adjustments to our household budget. I followed Gramm-Rudman procedures in my quest for the perfect tan. I decided that the family's grocery allotment could be slashed in half. We could also cut down on such non-essentials as heating fuel and electricity if push came to shove. When my family would see the benefits of my savage, tropical tan, no sacrifice would be too great.

The road to glamour and a tanned hide is not necessarily without its potholes. Using a tanning bed is comparable to being the lead character in Edgar Allen Poe's "The Premature Burial". It is definitely not for people suffering from claustrophobia.

After I had filled out a questionaire about my past medical history and had more or less waived the pool from any legal proceedings in the event all of my skin would fall off, I was ushered into a small room which contained the tanning bed. It looked like an elongated microwave oven with a collapsible lid.

One of our daughters, who apparently is much more informed about such matters, had told me that the best way to use the bed was au naturel. For several good reasons, I chose to recline on the bed modestly attired in my one-piece bathing suit. For one reason, there are vast portions of my body which have not been exposed to the light of day for as long as I can remember. Also, I considered the possibility of a fire breaking out in the pool building, which would necessitate a hasty departure from the premises. I decided that I would run the risk of having tan lines over being embarrassed in the presence of our town's entire voluntary fire department.

After my clothing change, I inserted two tokens into the machine. The brightest lights I have ever seen appeared on the inside cover and bottom layer of the casket-like bed. Taking this as my cue to soak up the rays, I assumed the best tanning position possible on the bed and pulled down its lid.

For 26 minutes I basked in the unseasonal warmth of the tanning bed. It may have been snowing and sleeting outside, but inside the bed, I was being transported into the summer months. It was the best of all worlds, without bombardments of mosquitoes and pesky flies. As my skin slowly reached the parboil point, the images of summer came back to me: melting icecubes in tall, frosted glasses of lemonade, the coconutty smells of tanning oils and the gently lapping of water on a lake dock.

All too soon, my 26 minutes came to an end. As I dressed before the room's full-length mirror, I was satisfied to see that my skin had achieved a rosy glow. Within minutes, my car was slip-sliding down the icy highway toward home, and the distance increased between me and our town's answer to a time machine.

My Dreams of Becoming a Lady

Another birthday is only two days away and I have abandoned most hopes of ever becoming a lady. My earliest role models of ladies were Mamie Eisenhower and the perfect mothers on the television screen, Harriet Nelson and June Cleaver.

At an early age I knew that I was destined for a life of freshly ironed aprons and housedresses, precocious children with shining faces and an organized file of the latest recipes. My dream house would have a white picket fence and climbing roses and would never be less than immaculate.

I would wear a string of pearls and high heels when I did my housework. My leisure-filled afternoons would be spent entertaining other ladies at coffee parties where I would preside at the silver service. Weekly appointments at the beauty parlor would receive top priority.

Somehow I missed the mark. I don't own an apron and I have yet to find a pair of high heels which don't cut off my circulation. My recipe filing system leaves much to be desired and our home is constantly in a state of disrepair because of remodeling.

I still harbor fantasies about becoming a lady someday. Some morning, when I least expect it, I will wake up as a changed person. My closet will be filled to overflowing with smart beige ensembles and my fingernails will be perfectly manicured. I will wear simple gold chains wherever I go and vichyssoise and chicken cordon bleu will replace my tired casserole dishes which are based on cream of mushroom soup.

My decisions to reject or accept invitations will make or break the parties. When I decide to attend parties, I will be able to talk brilliantly about the latest plays and authors of best-sellers. With my beige clothes, gold chain, poise and witty charm, I would dazzle everyone.

Some necessary steps will have to be taken before my dreams of becoming a lady will materialize, however. For one thing, someone I know will have to give a party. My favorite jeans and t-shirts will have to be discarded. Of course, my manicured nails will not allow for gardening, washing the dishes or washing the cars.

My hectic social calendar would leave me little time to bake cookies or to prepare dinners using ground beef in 100 different ways.

With my time-consuming roles as a wife, mother and teacher, it would be almost impossible to assume another role at the moment. It appears that my ambition to become a lady will have to be indefinitely shelved with my other juvenile hopes of becoming a fireman, a private detective or an interpreter for the United Nations.

Dressed to Kill

Except for one embarrassing oversight, our first holiday party of the season was a success. It was our first attempt at group entertaining since our second daughter graduated from high school last spring. It was also sheer luck that I was able to relocate the ice bucket, the guest towels and the one good tablecloth that doesn't sport food stains.

Some of our tablecloths have gone through so many food spills that they resemble gigantic scratch-and-sniff stickers.

No energy was spared in preparing our home for the evening's festivities. The ironing board was removed from the middle of our bedroom, where it has stood at attention since the basement flooded last summer. After a flurry of excitement, the vacuum cleaner was found exactly where I had left it last September. The mountain of shoes left on the back porch was relegated to the appropriate closets.

By the time I had finished dusting, vacuuming, cooking and hiding the glasses with dishwasher marks, I was left with 13 minutes to take a shower and get dressed before the first guest would arrive.

The dress I chose to wear was one I had borrowed from a sister eight years ago and had intended to return the next week. Although she refers to it affectionately as her "fat dress", I tend to think of it as a lifesaver. It's long, black and roomy. Whenever I wear it, I feel like Beverly Sills. Outside of the camp tee-shirts left over from my Girl Scout leader days, it's the most elegant thing hanging in my closet.

The long, black dress is capable of covering a multitude of sins. Because it's so roomy, it could be worn by virtually anyone; a pregnant woman, a watermelon smuggler, or even a columnist with a penchant for pizza. Within the confines of my favorite black dress, Ma Kettle could have been mistaken for Raquel Welch. The dress is a miracle.

As the first guest could be heard arriving at our back door, I pulled on the dress without a second to spare. I didn't have time to do my three standard poses in front of the full-length mirror in order to capture the full effect of my now willowy figure.

The guests began streaming into our house, and there were coats to be stored away, introductions to make and food to be served. Many of the guests smiled at me in a special way as I fluttered from one room to another in my smart, black gown. I smiled back. It was a delightful time and it was proving to be well worth all of the extra effort.

When the evening's activities were in full swing, I experienced my moment of truth. While I balanced a dish of food in one hand, and I was retelling one of my favorite anecdotes for the hundredth time, I happened to glance down at my elegant, black gown. I froze in suspended animation and realized why I had been the recipient of so many smiles that evening.

My favorite black dress was inside out.

The Bathing Suit Dilemma

Once again, I am faced with my annual decision: whether or not to wear a bathing suit on public beaches this summer.

Each spring I take a long, hard look at myself in a full-length mirror and rate what I see on a scale of 1-10. A one indicates that I should be able to wedge myself into a suit; a ten implies a walking disaster area. When I see a ten looming in the mirror, I know that there isn't enough elastic in the world to cover the proof of my eating habits.

A ten placed on any public beach is not a pretty picture. Innocent bystanders shield their eyes with their hands and small children run screaming for their mothers.

It makes no difference to them that I only eat to celebrate. I eat what is offered to me when people get married, when they have babies, or if there is a funeral. I've noticed that when people celebrate, they never say, "My wife just had a baby. Have a toothpick!" Rather, they force you to eat a chocolate candy bar and someone else bakes a cake for the occasion.

Not only do I help celebrate special occasions, but I also celebrate Mondays, Wednesdays and Fridays. I am probably the only person who celebrates John Quincy Adams' birthday or the day that Hiawatha speared his first fish. In my personal calendar of special events, everyday is a cause for celebration.

Considering the fact that potato chip manufacturers came out with at least half a dozen new flavors and textures this year, I thought the bathing suit companies would take such factors into consideration when they designed this year's models.

Instead, they defied the odds and came out with some styles for this summer which leave very little to the imagination. In an attempt to give every woman the illusion of having long, willowy legs, they have openings above the outer thighs which run almost to the armpits. The deep, plung-ing necklines extend beyond the navel. The new bathing suit styles seem appropriate for about two percent of the female population. They are not intended for victims of varicose veins, stretch marks or thunder thighs.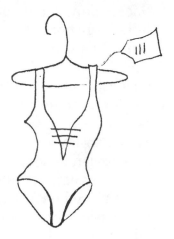

The new suits are not designed for women who like to celebrate. They are not in-tended for potato chip afi-cionados and people who can't turn down a baby shower. Rather, they are meant for a pitiful group of melancholy women with acute chloresterol and chocolate deficiencies.

How I pity them. If this summer, I see one of those emaciated creatures on the beach, while I am walking around enshrouded in a beach towel, I will do what any understanding person would do. I'll offer her a potato chip.

I'm Short for my Weight

"Older men report themselves as being taller and heavier than they actually are, and older women say they are taller but lighter." (From the Metropolitan Life Insurance Company's Statistical Bulletin)

Why on earth would men want people to think they weigh more than they actually do? Like those older women, I would like people to think I weigh less.

I reached my ideal weight when I was 12 years old. Ever since then, I have blatantly lied about my weight to doctors, drivers' license bureaus and insurance salesmen. In fact, I have been stretching the truth for so many years, that I'm no longer sure what I actually weigh.

All I know is that they no longer make accurate weight scales. Scales today are truly a disappointment. They cruelly exaggerate, and they fail to indicate my true weight which, in case you are interested, is 100 pounds.

I haven't had an honest weight listed on my driver's license since I received my driver's permit in 1957. If they handed out Academy Awards for the best acting performance in a license bureau, I would be a hands-down winner.

It doesn't help that the woman in charge of drivers' licenses wears a size three. There is no way that I can tell another woman, especially a thin woman, what the scales have been showing as my actual weight.

Granted, my weight has fluctuated over the years. There have been times when I may have resembled the Goodyear blimp, and there have been times when I could have balanced the scales with a three-quarter ton pickup truck. On the other hand, there have been times when I have gone perhaps two or three days without eating chocolate, and things have a way of balancing out.

My acting ability has enabled me to stand at the license renewal counter and to say without the blinking of an eye, "My weight? One hundred pounds, of course!" Debra Winger couldn't do it better.

Although my scale back home would indicate otherwise, and 100 pounds could more accurately describe the weight of one of my thighs, I continue in my deception.

Even if I had to be wedged through the doorway of the license bureau with the help of a crowbar, I would still insist that I weigh less.

As with any deception, there are rare occasions when I feel guilty about minimizing my weight. When I'm driving down the interstate and a truck weighing station looms ahead, indicating that all loads over 200,000 pounds should pull over, it takes all the strength I can muster to keep my car on the road.

When a clothing salesclerk bursts into gales of laughter after I ask for a size six, I feel compelled to sink to my knees and beg for forgiveness.

At times, the truth hurts.

Talking Bathroom Scales

If there's one thing I can live without this Christmas, it's a talking bathroom scale. According to a Christmas catalog, this electronic marvel records and announces your weight at the touch of a button. A five-person memory bank is capable of storing the weights for an entire family.

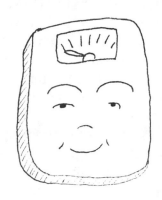

In my opinion, the manufacturers of bathroom scales have overstepped the line of good judgment this year. As if it wasn't bad enough to read our actual weights, we now have scales shouting the numbers out for all to hear.

I have always considered weighing myself to be a private act, tantamount to removing ear wax or weaving dental floss between my molars. Standing on a bathroom scale was never intended to be a spectator sport. In fact, one of the main factors in determining the size of our family was my bashful reluctance to weigh myself in the presence of doctors and nurses.

I never weigh myself when another person is in the house, out of sheer fear that someone will look over my shoulder and read the numbers. My favorite weighing place is the walk-in bedroom closet, where, if I chin myself on a clothes rod while standing on the scale, my weight is somewhere between 35 and 40 pounds.

Imagine the horror of standing on a talkative scale which is capable of shouting out, "You weigh 170 pounds!", and its voice reverberates from every wall in the house. I also doubt whether I would care to have other people tap into my memory bank and discover my gains and losses for the past week.

A talking scale with a memory could be a dangerous thing. If its batteries allow it to talk and have a memory, what will keep it from becoming a malicious gossip as well? It could prove to be disconcerting to have a scale announce, "You weigh 170 pounds. Do you realize you outweigh everyone else in your family?" A few comments like that, and our country might witness a wave of criminal assaults on bathroom scales.

A scale which can announce weights can also issue insults. Imagine this scenario. It's Christmas Day and you have just overdosed on turkey, ham, mashed potatoes, and several varieties of pie. You waddle off to the scale in order to access the damage. The scale wheezes as you step onto it and then lets out an audible groan.

"Ye gads," extolls the scale, "you really did it this time, didn't you? Your present weight, to put it subtly, is exactly the same as a Mack truck." (You hear nervous twitters of laughter in the nearby living room as your friends and family members eavesdrop on the high-tech conversation.) "If you keep this up," continues the scale, "you will soon be a fat lady in a circus."

Imagine this scene replayed in thousands of bathrooms across the country. This may be state-of-the-art, but no, thanks.

I would rather take my chances on an old, silent scale, where the jumpy indicator needle moves each time you shift your weight and the results are rarely accurate. When you weigh yourself, ignorance can be bliss.

Great Expectations

There is very little that we wouldn't do for our daughters. However, a recent news article has caused me to reconsider exactly how far we could be pushed. I would like to make one thing perfectly clear to them: I will not have their children.

A 48-year-old woman in Johannesburg recently gave birth to her own grandchildren. After the triplets were born, the woman noted, "If I make my daughter happy, then I will be happy too."

Personally, I would rather buy my daughters some new sweaters or bake some cookies for  them. I would prefer to walk over hot coals or have root canal surgery if it would make them happy.

At times I have been pregnant and at other times I haven't been pregnant, and I must admit that not being pregnant was better. Maybe I feel that way because I never felt that certain glow, which allegedly accompanies every pregnancy. If any woman past childbearing age says that a pregnancy is the most wonderful time in one's life, she probably forgets other things too.

Each of my four pregnancies lasted at least 11 months. By the time the girls were born, they were the size of 3-month-olds and they were walking and talking.

During each of the four pregnancies, I ate as though there were no tomorrow. I was bulimic long before the word became fashionable. The only difference was that I didn't make myself sick afterwards. As a result of my propensity for eating everything in sight, I became a walking human blimp. If I would have painted the word Goodyear on my sides, tourists would have gone crazy.

I would eat right out of the refrigerator. While most pregnant women eat for two, I ate enough to feed a family of 12. My husband once observed that I was probably the only woman alive who got tan from a refrigerator light. The only glow I ever felt was the direct result of heartburn.

My mind stayed relatively intact but my body went berserk. My feet were the size of footballs and my figure became gargantuan. I would think twice about sitting down anyplace, because it meant getting back up again.

Other people were quick to notice my unsightly figure. Instead of the usual "Oh, you're going to have a baby!", I usually heard gasps of horror and disbelief. "Wow! Are you ever huge!" was probably the closest I ever came to receiving a compliment.

No, my darling daughters, think again if you are entertaining any ideas about me having your babies. I hope that the woman in South Africa hasn't given you any false hopes about having the best of two worlds: a baby and a perfect figure. When the time comes for you to have children, I'll be there with some freshly baked cookies.

Them

I never intended to grow older. However, when we visited our oldest daughters at their respective colleges this fall, I suddenly realized that I had become a middle-aged person. Somewhere along the way, when I wasn't paying attention, I became one of Them.

I had hoped to beat the odds, but this growing older business apparently is a genetic trait in our family. When I was quite young, and my grandparents were the age that I am now, the term "middle-aged" was synonymous with "ancient". If my grandparents would have told me that they had once cruised with Cleopatra down the Nile, fought dinosaurs or that they had come over on the Mayflower, I would have believed them.

When my parents slipped into their forties, they, too, began exhibiting signs of having stepped into the great beyond. They began calling their children by the wrong names, and they began getting shorter. They began babbling incessantly about little, inconsequential things, such as the rising costs of groceries, incidents from World War II, and how rock and roll music was going to ruin our eardrums. When I saw what they had become, I vowed that I would never get that old. I would learn from their mistakes.

This fall, we attended Parents' Day at our second daughter's college and I was "ma'am"ed more times than I care to remember. We engaged in obligatory conversations with her dormitory friends and those talks were liberally sprinkled with "Nice to meet you, Ma'am" and "How do you do, sir?" They all reminded me of Wally Cleaver's friend, Eddie Haskell, when he would ask, "And how are you today, Mrs. Cleaver?"

In their minds, we had apparently passed over into another world as far as age was concerned. I was tempted to grab one of them by the collar of his or her alligator sweater and yell out, "Hey, I'm not prehistoric, you know! I'm really young! I'm not as old as I look!"

Fortunately, I exercised some restraint, and realized that such an outburst would only confirm their worst suspicions about the doddering minds of middle-aged people.

Without much warning, I have become my grandmother and my mother. One morning I simply woke up and discovered that I was wearing a 46-year-old's body.

I had imagined that if I would keep up with the times, I would somehow manage to escape the middle-aged syndrome. As a teacher, I am aware of the language and attitudes of young people. I have tried to keep an open mind about changing social attitudes.

I did not clutch my heart when I discovered that our two daughters were living in coed dormitories with coed bathrooms. I don't panic when I read that high school students in St. Paul are staging protests because they want to wear hats in school and have cigarette breaks between classes.

How I became a middle-aged person will always be a mystery, but there is one thing that I do know for sure. If one more carry-out boy at the grocery store calls me "ma'am", I will hit him with my purse.

I Sing the Praises of Shoulder Pads

When I discovered shoulder pads, a new world of high fashion opened up to me. Like so many other women today, I have been transformed from a weak-shouldered shape into a fairly impressive imitation of Seattle Seahawk linebacker Brian Bosworth.

The best part about shoulder pads is that they make your waist look smaller. On the other hand, when people see a woman walking toward them with shoulders like the Incredible Hulk, they often neglect to see the rest of the body.

The slenderizing effect of shoulder pads is obvious. Take a good look at a professional football player, who is seldom seen in public without his shoulder pads. While it's a known fact that some of those bruisers weigh over 250 pounds, their shoulder pads make their waists look tiny by comparison. In order to maintain those pounds, there's also a good chance that they are eating more for breakfast than a piece of melba toast and half a grapefruit.

By slipping on a pair of shoulder pads, any woman today can have the swimming shoulders of Esther Williams without the bother of getting into a pool for daily workouts.

If wearing shoulder pads still leaves you with the appearance of a large pear, try wearing two sets of shoulder pads. Of course, your neck might run the risk of disappearing altogether, but your waist will definitely seem smaller. For hard-to-handle cases, I would suggest tying a fluffy bed pillow over each shoulder. Such an arrangement would also guarantee you front row status at any clearance sale rack. No one would want to mess around with a woman with such intimidating shoulders.

The only problem with shoulder pads is their tendency to shift. One unplanned movement with your shoulders could do considerable damage to your fashionable image. You may leave the house in the morning, with perfectly balanced shoulders, but by noon you may resemble Quasimoto, the hunchback of Notre Dame.

It's virtually impossible to control shoulder pads once they are determined to meander their way down your front or back. In a crowded office, or other workplace, some real sleight of hand is required to give your shoulder pads the necessary adjustments. If you should decide to throw caution to the wind and wear the shoulder pads slightly askew, your co-workers might start a collection to pay for your corrective surgery.

Shoulder pads for women appear to run in cycles. Forty years ago, Joan Crawford wouldn't have made a film without them. If the cycle should run true to form, we shouldn't have to worry about shoulder pads and the risks of looking like lopsided bodybuilders until the year 2029. By then, most of us will be too old to care.

The Rummage Sale

A company has admitted that it overcharged the Navy when it sold aircraft ashtrays for $660 each. On the other hand, the company has justified charging $2,710 for a lock. The company has agreed to reduce the price of the ashtrays from $660 to $50. In defense of the company and the Navy, I would like to observe from firsthand experience that setting prices can be an absolute dilemma.

Our family is preparing for our first rummage sale of the summer. Rather, I have been rummaging through boxes of castoffs from my family, running around the house with pieces of masking tape in my hair and on the backs of my hands, and acting like the madwoman of Chaillot. My family is trying to survive the experience.

It's a real challenge to establish fair prices for toys long discarded by the girls, clothes which they can no longer wear and the miscellaneous clutter which can accumulate after 23 years of marriage.

As if price setting was not enough to tax my mind, I must contend with the input of my family as each item is labeled with a handwritten price tag. Whether it's a Nehru jacket or a pair of bell-bottom jeans, the general reaction is that I have priced many of their old objects far too low. As I sort out the things which will be sold at the garage sale and those items which will be relegated to the trash can, their protests become even more vehement.

"Hey! Who threw this Barbie doll in the trash?"

After I explain that the beloved doll is in fact missing most of her hair and one leg, I still cannot shrug off the feeling that I have been viewed as some type of executioner.

The fact that I have scheduled a rummage sale one week away has had a remarkable effect on the values systems of those dearest to me. Boxes of clothing which have been abandoned on the top shelves of closets have been discovered to contain "my favorite cut-offs", "my favorite shirt" or "my best jeans".

The girls, who seemingly have been more concerned with hour-long phone calls and the excitement of their teen years, wince as I cold-heartedly set aside their old toys, tricycles, read-to-me books and too small ice-skates for the Big Sale.

The girls are "keepers" in a world where their mother has the theory that if an object hasn't been used during the past year, it's a likely candidate for a rummage sale. As I burrow through the endless boxes armed with the masking tape and my felt-tip pen, I can survey these objects from our past with passive detachment.

Perhaps the military suppliers were not able to price their goods with the same objectivity. Maybe they had grown overly sentimental about their ashtrays. Investigations might show that the company officials had had mothers rummaging off their favorite things when they were young.

Numbers

Numbers are easy for some people. If the theory is valid about one half of us being controlled by an analytical half of our brain and the other half being creative, these people would belong to the former group.

These people have memorized their Social Security numbers and driver's license numbers and can tell you, without blinking an eye, the birthdates and ages of their children.

They can instantly figure out the effect of a 25 percent sale on a $14.99 purchase. They can mentally compute, within an error margin of 15 cents, their purchases in a grocery store.

Unfortunately, this has not been my life story. I have caused much embarrassment for members of my family when I have turned up several dollars short at check-out counters. My husband will never cease to be appalled at my creative mathematics while balancing the checkbook.

Whenever called upon for my Social Security number, I have to fumble through a two-inch thick pack of identification cards. The only way that I can remember my age is to subtract the year I was born from the present year.

Numbers are an immense bother. Cutting a recipe down to half proportions can send me into an absolute frenzy. Try though I might, it is simply impossible to figure out one-half of 3/8 teaspoon. Because of my mathematical inabilities, we often have chili or lasagna for as long as four days in a row.

Directory assistance personnel have no patience with people like me. It's definitely easier for them to rattle off a 10-digit long distance telephone number than it is for me to write it down. With the advance of automated voices which state the given number once and then repeat it only once, I find myself redialing directory assistance several times in order to get the correct number.

If a "real person" is handling directory assistance, he or she becomes immediately incensed when I ask for a number to be repeated. It makes me wonder whether they have creative sides to their brains.

Life became much easier for me when we moved from a complicated street address to a plain old rural route. We kept the amount of our children down to a manageable number to recall. I've been married to one man and, if given enough time to think about it, I can also tell you that we have been married for 22 years. Or is it 23?

I doubt whether I will ever become some sort of mathematical wizard at this stage of my life. Armed with a well-used pocket calculator and a passable sense of humor, I will simply have to survive in a world seemingly dominated with left-brained people. Or is it the right brain?

Who's the Boss?

The phone rang and our second daughter, who is on the high school track team and tends to answer the phone first, called out, "It's a man and he wants to talk to the boss!"

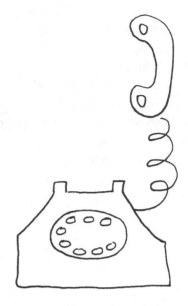

"Get your dad" was my resigned reply.

We have been married for almost 28 years and it has taken me at least that long to understand the labels given to husbands and wives by other people.

When people ask me about "the old man", "the boss", "the chief" or "the mister", I now know that they are referring to my husband. It took me a long time to realize that the "old man" was not my father and "the boss" was not my principal at the school where I teach.

Perhaps the name for my husband that bothers me the most is "your better half". My better half of what? Whenever I hear that expression, I think about a cartoon I saw several years ago. One woman in the cartoon was seen whispering to her friend, "They're a nice couple except for her".

Women are designated with other epithets: "the little lady", "the lady of the house", "the little woman", "the old lady" and "the missus". "The lady of the house" makes me feel like the owner of a bordello, "the missus" reminds me of the ante-bellum South and "little woman" rings of Louisa May Alcott.

During the spring we have more than our share of

door-to-door salesmen. They come up to our farmhouse door hawking Bibles, farm tools and encyclopedias. The salesmen typically travel in dusty cars and vans with out-of-state license plates and they speak with syrupy southern drawls.

This spring was no exception. When I answered the knock at the door, I was greated by a young man, who was carrying a load of books under one arm and fending off our affectionate collie with the other.

"Howdy, ma'am. Could it be that I am speaking to the little lady of the house?"

It was a redundant question. He could have known by a quick glance at our streaked windows that I wasn't the cleaning lady. Or the maid. Or an attractive unmarried daughter. What seemed most preposterous to me was that a size twelve would be referred to as "little". I have never been little. Statuesque maybe, or even amazonian, but hardly "little".

What bothers me the most, I guess, is that we lose our real names and are given labels. The labels convey tired, old stereotypes and misconceptions about the roles of men and women. Women are seen as being passive and little, while men are the bosses and the aggressors.

Someday I would like to respond to the phone caller who asks, "Is the boss there?" I would love to answer, "Speaking."

Someday I will risk the outcome and find the courage.

The Pantyhose Problem

Pantyhose are 30 years old. Although I have never owned a pair that has lasted longer than one week, the one-piece undergarment first appeared in our stores in 1959.

According to the legend, Allen Gant, a mill president in the late 1950's, asked his wife, "How would it be if we made a pair of panties and fastened the stockings to it?" Ethel, his wife, gave him the go-ahead.

Because of Ethel and Allen, modern women no longer have to contend with snapping nylons to lumpy garter belts and girdles. We only have to worry about little things like slipped vertebrae and wrenched back muscles.

It would appear that pantyhose were invented under the mistaken idea that women are contortionists. Most women will agree that inserting the first leg into a pair of pantyhose is a relatively simple matter. However, once one leg is finished, getting the second leg into the hose is a death-defying act.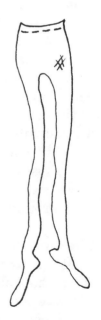

The only way this feat can be accomplished is to hop around the bedroom on one foot and hope that the suspended leg will somehow land up in the right position without toppling over.

Training in yoga is essential to putting on pantyhose within a reasonable length of time unless, of course, you are accustomed to wrapping one of your legs around your neck. The possibility also exists that after all of this work, a run will be discovered and the entire process will have to be repeated.

Another problem with pantyhose is the size designation system used by hosiery companies. If a woman holds a Ph.D. and is a prudent reader, she may be able to decipher from the pantyhose package that a given pair is suitable for a person weighing between 120 and 175 pounds and standing between 60 and 68 inches tall.

One would assume that the hose inside the package would allow for quite a bit of flexibility, right? Wrong.

The average pair of pantyhose has the flexibility of a slab of concrete. Woe to the woman who places her trust in the pantyhose sizing system. She might land up with the waistband pulled up to her neck, or it might only go as far up as her knees.

About four years ago, as I was dressing for work, I inadvertently put on a pair of my daughters' pantyhose (size A and designed for the piteously petite), thinking that they were my size B (designed for the basically broad). As my morning at work began, I became aware of my dilemma. The size A pantyhose, which once had come up to my waist, were succumbing to the theory of gravity and were slowly inching their way downward.

By the end of my second class, the waistband of the pantyhose had continued its travels and had bound my knees together. I was experiencing true stress as I hobbled around the room correcting students' English papers and I tried to maintain some sense of decorum. With my knees fused together with stretch elastic, I must have resembled Quasimoto as I lurched up and down the aisles of the classroom.

It was the longest day of my life and I owed it all to Allen Gant, the founder of pantyhose.

The VCR

I only have nodding acquaintances with our household appliances. They might have developed into deep relationships if I only would have taken the time to read the instruction manuals that came with them.

Although our microwave oven supposedly has fourteen functions and two memory banks, I have only been able to use it as a hot dog cooker. I once tried reading the instruction booklet, but I couldn't get past the table of contents.

The language was simply too technical. After I rifled through the pages, which described setting the timer and how to push the function pads, it became obvious that only an electrical engineer would be capable of making a complete meal with a microwave oven.

This week I decided to have a head-on confrontation with our VCR machine. The ominous-looking machine has served chiefly as a dust collector since Christmas of last year. On a few occasions, when my hus-  band and I have felt adventurous and devil-may-care, we have rented movies for the machine and have seen them with few mishaps.

On the day in question, I decided to record a horror movie which would be viewed at 1 a.m. that night. After looking through the manual's table of contents, it seemed most likely that my course of action would be a one-touch timer recording with a delayed start. To this day, I have no idea what that means. After I scanned the illustrated instructions, it soon became clear that one-touch means touching twenty-odd buttons and dials in the proper sequence.

Halfway through the complicated instructions, I could no longer be certain whether I was making a video tape or building an atomic bomb. For all I knew, our house would self-destruct when I pushed the final button.

I set start and end times, a button labeled counter-timer and several other buttons with obscure abbreviations printed on them. After the instruction booklet no longer seemed to correspond to what I was doing, I cast it aside, and began pushing more buttons in reckless abandon. When every possible light on the machine began blinking in dizzy array, I decided that my job was finished.

I went to bed that night, unsure whether I would be recording the horror movie or an exercise program beamed in from a Russian satellite. Although I couldn't be sure what I had done, I trusted that the machine, with all of its delicate circuitry and blinking lights, would somehow read my mind and come through with the right program.

Imagine my disappointment the next morning, when the lights could still be seen blinking and there was no movie. It seems that during my unorthodox approach to recording a movie, I had neglected to follow the first instruction which read, "Load a cassette tape into the machine." The machine had apparently followed my directions to the letter and had recorded the movie in-to thin air.

I have learned one important lesson through this experience, however. If a machine or appliance comes with an instruction booklet, it's best to leave it alone.

The Frump

I didn't realize I was a frump until this week. It was also a great surprise to read that we have been organized into a national organization.

The National Frumps of America is based in Winter Park, Fla. The group even has its own acronym, FRUMP: Frugal, responsible, unpretentious, mature personality.

Frump fashions include sensible crepe-soled shoes, pearls and elasticized waistbands. Frumps like to do sensible things like converting gallon bleach bottles into hanging plant baskets and bird feeders.

I haven't gone quite that far. Although the most creative thing I do around the house is cook up an occasional batch of prepackaged macaroni and cheese, my attire certainly gives me away as a card-carrying member of FRUMP.

When my spinal disks began rubbing together and making noises like castanets, I turned to crepe-soled shoes. While wearing the crepe soles in the classroom, I also discovered an unexpected bonus. I could steal up behind my students, while they were taking tests, and scare the wits out of them. Crepe soles seemed to satisfy my basically inherent sadistic streak.

My tastes in clothing have always been eclectic. At some unrecorded time in my life, I stopped wearing my mother's hand-me-downs and began wearing my daughters' discards.

What I wear each day is pretty well determined by what's on top of the clothes basket in the laundry room.

I was mixing plaids with stripes long before the fashion magazines thought of it. While they refer to the look as being versatile, whimsical and dashing, I have always thought of it as being practical. My clothes fall somewhere in the grey area between garage sale and rag bag.

Elasticized waistbands have been a godsend. My body has yo-yoed between widespread sizes for most of my adult life.

With the exception of tent dresses, elasticized waistbands have done what few clothing features have been able to do. During the blimp stages of my life, they have allowed me to wear clothing and to breathe at the same time.

If being a frump means dressing comfortably, I plead guilty.

Ma'am? No Thanks!

For a few brief seconds last week, I was a man. At least I was perceived to be a man and it was a very unsettling experience.

Granted, my hair is short this summer and gender mistakes could be made. With men running around in ponytails and earrings, confusion of this sort is understandable.

I had pulled my car into a gas station and the attendant came running out to greet me. That incident alone would be worth another column. I thought that running out to cars in gas stations had gone the way of 25-cent a gallon gas and free premiums with car-fills.

"May I help you, sir?" he asked breathlessly. Then he saw my face. He quickly realized the error of his ways and amended his original greeting. "Oh, I'm sorry, ma'am!" he stammered.

It was the first time in my life that I had ever been "sir"-ed, and I must admit that there is a distinct difference between being "sir"-ed and being "ma'am"-ed. There were different inflections in his voice when the attendant spoke.

"Sir" reminds me of noble causes, and it carries with it an air of certain respect.

"Ma'am" smacks of the Old West, and it reminds me of Miss Kitty at the "Gunsmoke" saloon. Loosely translated into cowboy language, "ma'am" meant, "Ha, ha, ha. I'm carrying a gun and you aren't." It was a real putdown.

I'm sure that if any cowpokes ever "ma'am"-ed Annie Oakley or Calamity Jane, they didn't live to talk about it.

"Ma'am" seems more condescending than "sir". I wasn't "ma'am"-ed until my 40th birthday, and until then I was addressed as "miss".

To this day, whenever I'm "ma'am"-ed, I feel as

though I should be carrying a Pekingese dog and be traipsing off to the opera. Today, "ma'am" seems to be synonymous with "rusty relic".

I would much rather be addressed by men as an equal, if not more. "Your Highness" has a nice ring to it, and I'm sure that Princess Grace was never offended by the title.

One thing is for sure. If a carryout person at a grocery store would call me "Your Highness", I would buy all of my groceries there.

The Plumber

For the past two weeks, I have been pursuing another man.

I call him repeatedly on the phone, and he rarely returns my calls. He has only visited our cottage twice and I fear that I may never see him again.

The man is a plumber and I must admit that I have exhausted my supply of feminine wiles to keep him around. I haven't made such a fool of myself over a man since I sent a let- 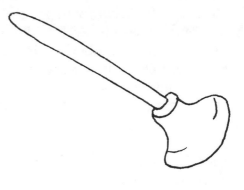 ter to Elvis Presley in 1957 and pledged my undying love and devotion.

He showed up at our door soon after I placed a call to the plumber with the most attractive ad in the yellow pages. It was a Monday morning and I was in desperate need of someone to install a washing machine and a water softener and to correct some basement plumbing which tends to erupt like Mt. Vesuvius after each spring thaw.

At noon he left for some emergencies, and he didn't return until Friday afternoon shortly before quitting time.

In my way of thinking, not having a washing machine is an emergency. I can't imagine what con- stitutes an emergency to a plumber, except maybe res- cuing someone who is floating face down in a toilet.

Based on the population surrounding the lakes dur- ing the summer, there simply can't be enough

47

emergencies to keep a plumber away for days at a time.

His last words to me last Friday were, "I don't know when I'll be back." As he shrugged his shoulders, he reminded me of Humphrey Bogart. Those words coming from the mouth of a plumber are as fully spine-chilling as having a dentist tell you, "Your gums have to be removed.

I have decided that I will go to almost any extreme to have wash-rinse-spin cycles like other women. If and when I see the plumber again, he should be advised that he will be dealing with the black widow spider of plumbing customers.

I'll entice him with cookies and coffee, even though I haven't bothered to bake cookies for my family for years. I will offer to mend his socks or even make his dinner for him. If all else fails, I will hold him as a captive in our basement until the work is done.

It shouldn't be all that difficult to tether him to the electric water heater when he least expects it. I'll give him enough rope to work on the water lines and I'll not let him go until the work is completed, or he becomes eligible for Social Security, or whichever comes first. I'm willing to be flexible.

Until I can hear the washing machine click through its cycles, he will live like a mole-person in our basement. All's fair in love and plumbing.

As I see it, he had a chance to say "no" when I first called, reciting my litany of plumbing needs. If he would have simply said, "I'm sorry, but I'm all booked up so please call another plumber," things could have been different. My hopes and water pipes wouldn't have been left dangling in thin air.

Unless this plumbing fiasco is cleared up, there will be no more Mrs. Nice Guy.

The Scorch Factor

Move over, windchill factors and dew points.

Television and radio weather reports in Arizona, Georgia and Texas are now giving us something else to worry about: the "scorch factor."

The scorch factor indicates how long it will take the sun's altraviolet rays to start burning unprotected skin.

In light of the fact that it may be winter before this index is finally released to the northern states, I would like to take this opportunity to share my own list of tanning danger signals.

This is only a partial list of symptoms that I've experienced during decades of basting, roasting and rotating in the sun.

There have been times in my life when I have identified more with a Thanksgiving turkey on a spit than a bronzed beauty.

In fact, I have always envied those holiday birds with their built-in pop-up timers. You rarely see a turkey that's peeling.

For what it is worth, here is my list. You know you have had enough sun when:

You get up from your blanket at the beach and your back is left behind, sticking to the blanket.

A family of five next to you asks if they may use your back to grill their hamburgers.

You walk into a room and the air conditioner kicks on.

You walk into church and all the candles melt.

Complete strangers grab your hands and offer you their condolences.

You're lying in the sun and hear fat sizzling, and you know it's not bacon.

Small children walk up and ask if they may peel you.

People take one look at you and the topic of conversation suddenly switches to talk about obscure leper colonies.

You feel compelled to stick your head in a hot oven in order to cool off.

Your entire body feels like a discarded pile of crinkled crepe.

Bird watchers ask if you are in your molting season.

Unless you're lucky enough to be like a turkey with a pop-up timer, be careful out there.

The Exercise Bike

I have always been suspicious of people who are obsessed with physical fitness. It's hard to trust them when they tell you they have doubled their heart rates and that it feels good. Gasping for breath and perspiration have never really fit into my particular lifestyle.

For most of my adult life, my personal exercise program consisted of moving a fork around on a plate of food and walking from the living room to the kitchen during commercials. If I ever felt a little wild and crazy, I might bend over and tie my shoelaces or tear open a bag of potato chips. I had grown used to muscles which felt like fresh marshmallows.

My husband and I recently decided to invest in some sort of exercise equipment. In case you haven't noticed, exercise machines today bear a striking resemblance to medieval torture devices. The cross country skiing machines, the rowing machines and stationary bicycles are finished in flat black paint and they are all rather ominous looking.

The only features conspiculously missing on exercise equipment today are sharp metal spikes and thumbscrews. I wouldn't be surprised to see the eventual comeback of the rack, that Middle Ages favorite which pulled its victim's limbs out of place.

We finally settled on a stationary bicycle, which would at least allow us to be seated comfortably while we succumbed to the inevitable pain. So far, I have had a love-hate relationship with the machine. It looms like a monster in our spare bedroom and although its manual guarantees us "a lifetime of health", it has come to represent exquisite torture and all that is wrong with the world. Philosophically speaking, a stationary bicycle is much like life: you pedal as fast as you can without getting anywhere.

If being healthy means having knotted muscles and

gasping for air, I should live for ages. After my first ride on the bike, it felt as though large grapefruit had been implanted up and down my legs. After the second ride, I could no longer feel my legs at all. I was mercifully numbed from the waist down.

The owner's manual advised us to adjust the tension so that it would be comfortable. It soon became clear that comfortable tension is a contradiction in terms. The lightest tension on the bike might be comfortable for a trained Olympic athlete or a Marine, but it would be easier for me to wade through a mixer of wet concrete.

I can finally pedal for three miles without having legs which feel like rubber and risking cardiac arrest. I try not to be discouraged by the mileages chalked up by other members of our household and the fact that they can smile and bicycle at the same time.

At my present endurance rate, I should be reaching four miles a day by the turn of the century. After each three-mile torture session, I kneel down, kiss the floor and give thanks that I'm still alive.

I never realized that feeling better could hurt quite so much.

Exercise

It's pretty easy to feel guilty about not getting exercise these days. It seems as though most of my friends are steadily defecting over to the "other side", by joining classes in aerobic dance and aquarobics. They swim laps at the community pool before the sun comes up in the morning, bicycle around town and are filling their closets with cute, color-coordinated jogging suits and running shoes.

After countless years of picking up toys around the house and running up and down the stairs with the laundry, I was actually looking forward to this time of my life, when I would be able to just sit. For years I looked forward to the time when I would be able to sit back and do crossword puzzles to my 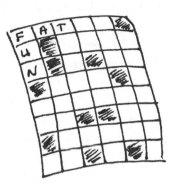 heart's content and read exotic novels which would carry me to all parts of the world and back through history. Sitting down and doing nothing was a luxury that I figured I deserved.

My friends assure me that if I would work up a lather by running or double my normal heart rate by dancing, I would feel better. Perhaps I'm a skeptic, but I suspect that they are more than slightly masochistic. It wouldn't surprise me if they would similarly extoll the virtues of poking bamboo slivers under their fingernails or walking barefoot through beds of hot coals.

I read a quote recently by a fellow cynic who stated that anyone who would tell you that jogging makes you feel better would probably lie about other things, too.

I try to avoid head-on confrontations with people with physical fitness fetishes, but that task is becoming increasingly difficult. They are everywhere. They show up at the bakery downtown after their morning swims and compare lap times over spartan cups of coffee, while I silently devour my daily allowance of doughnuts and try my best to blend in with the bakery wall panels.

They literally jog through the grocery stores, throwing granola, fresh vegetables and bags of whole wheat flour into their shopping carts. I am aware of their looks of disdain as they glance at my cart, which is usually filled to overflowing with junk food, ice cream and frozen pizzas.

Maybe they have reason to appear so smug. They most likely have healthy, gorgeously enlarged lungs and sinewy muscle development. The way they carry on, they will undoubtedly live for many more decades.

But there are the inevitable drawbacks for them, of course. Since they are so busy running, swimming and aerobic dancing, most of them would probably fail to come up with a three-letter word referring to the capital of Bashkir, USSR.

It is unlikely, too, that they would be able to boast of a clothes closet which contains clothing in sizes ten through fourteen. How I pity them.

Halloween Candy

I love chocolate. Through diets and weight loss programs, through thick and thin, my love for chocolate ranks right up there with the sanctity of life and loyalty to my country. If I had my way, chocolate would be declared the national food.

Even though I weigh considerably less than I did one year ago, I still entertain fantasies about being stranded on a desert island with a ton of chocolate. Because of my fondness for chocolate, I looked forward to this past Halloween with considerable fear and trepidation.

With ironclad resolve, I waited until the afternoon of October 31 to make my chocolate purchases at the grocery store. The first trick-or-treaters began arriving within two hours of my trip to the store. I now realize that I was hoping that all of those little people would be grounded by their parents and no one would ring our doorbell. I also reasoned that leftover chocolate would be a shame to waste.

My hidden hopes were dashed to the ground when a unicorn and two bunnies, all under three feet in height, made off with several of my miniature chocolate bars. As the doorbell rang nonstop for the next two hours, they were followed by pirates, vampires, ghosts and tiny punk rockers.

I realized finally, with a certain amount of horror, that my cache of chocolate had dwindled drastically. Only five candy bars, miserable-looking and begging to be eaten, remained on the bottom of the plastic pail. For a short time, I considered turning off the front porch light in hopes of discouraging any more pint-sized visitors to our door. I became convinced that the light was attracting them like millions of tiny moths. Millions of chocolate-eating moths.

After a few minutes, the quiet of the evening was broken by the sound of the doorbell. Miss America and her companion, a hobo, proceeded to reduce my collection by another two bars. At that moment of truth, their costumes seemed more ghastly and terrifying than any others I had seen.

With the defensiveness of a mother lion, I sat on the couch and guarded the remaining three bars as if they were my cubs. I gave serious thought to devouring the chocolate bars instantly and handing out items from the kitchen shelves to any stragglers still lurking outside our door. After all, what child wouldn't be delighted to receive a box of baking soda or a box of breakfast cereal?

As I look back on that evening, I also realize that my perceptions of small children changed dramatically as the night wore on. When I had a pail overflowing with chocolate candy bars, the first trick-or-treaters could be described as cute and charming. When the pail was half-full, they really appeared to be gremlins. When only three bars stood between me and the oncoming hordes, anyone ringing the doorbell had to be a downright thief.

As it turned out, no one else came to our door, demanding rights to my chocolates. Trick-or-treaters can cause a person much anxiety. When I'm anxious, I eat chocolate.

The Sweat Pants

I have always shied away from physical exertion. Given the choices in life it has always been pinochle over pumping iron and best-seller novels over jogging. I have always been leery of activities which tend to make a person sweat.

Although I am reluctant to double my heart rate through aerobic dancing, many of my friends and relatives have unwittingly succumbed to the physical fitness frenzy which is sweeping our country. One of our daughters runs up to four miles every day and another daughter can't relax until she has jumped rope 500 times. Through all of these activities I have remained patiently tolerant. I accept their fanaticism for physical exercise in much the same manner that other people have learned to accept skeletons in their family closets.

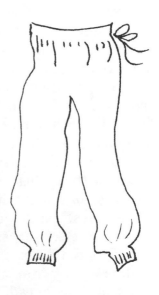

This summer I decided to change my public image. If I couldn't work out like them, I could at least dress like them. I have always marvelled at how physically fit some people look and I believe that much of their healthy appearance can be attributed to their sweatsuits, jogging shorts and running shoes. Even though they may have shin splints, torn ligaments and be gasping for breath, their attire says to all of the world, "Hey, look, I exercise!"

I chose a sporting goods shop which caters to the needs of runners, and I was overwhelmed by the displays of sweatbands, pedometers, flimsy nylon running suits and marathon posters. Although I consider myself to be an expert when it comes to choosing potato chips and other junk food, this was a new consumer experience.

A young, healthy looking woman came bounding up the aisle toward me. With her bronzed skin and carefully groomed muscles. She looked perfectly Amazonian.

Not wishing to appear as a novice in this new world of physical torture, I told her that I needed to replace my old sweat pants. I tried to look healthy and casual about the whole thing.

She led me to a table covered with sweat pants of ever imaginable color. It didn't take me long to realize that sweat pants come in three sizes: small, medium and "don't leave the house". I chose a navy blue pair in the latter size.

"Would you like to try these on?" asked the salesclerk, who was resembling Charles Atlas more and more as time passed. I quickly decided to buy the sweat pants without trying them on. I had no desire to entertain anyone in the store with a glimpse of my cellulite camouflaged in navy blue.

In the privacy of my home, with the curtains drawn and the door dead-bolted, I tried on my new purchase. The full-length mirror in our bedroom tells no lies, and it would be subtle to say that I looked like a large, plump blueberry. In fact, I bore a strong resemblance to one of those "before" photos in the diet center ads. So much for looking like an athlete.

The sweat pants have been retired to a bottom drawer of a dresser, safely out of sight. Along with a string bikini, also bought during a moment of weakness, they bear mute testimony to my belief that better days lie ahead.

The Diet

A weight loss program was inevitable. At first, my body's calls for help were subtle.

My usable wardrobe had dwindled down to three pieces of clothing and I was literally covered with bruises from walking into furniture. The last straw occurred when I became wedged in the doorway while walking from the kitchen to the dining room.

My husband told me that a diet should be easy for me because I had dieted so many other times. In order to prove his point, he got out his calculator and estimated that during our 25 years of marriage I had lost approximately 3,000 pounds.

My mother, upon hearing the news of my pending diet, said that she would include me in her prayers. Because she has watched my weight go up and down for the past 45 years, my diets and her prayers have given her a completely new insight into religion.

I have survived a wide range of dieting crazes. I have eaten synthetic meals made from soybeans and drunk gallons of water and powdered mixes. I have eaten enough greens to feed all the rabbits of the world.

At one time, I resorted to complete starvation. After seemingly endless agony and interminable suffering, that particular approach to dieting only lasted 15 minutes.

Once I was involved in the Weight Watcher program, the eating highlights of my day included tuna fish, turkey and large quantities of yogurt. I became so involved with measuring and weighing my food that my kitchen resembled the laboratory of some mad scientist.

When I switched from my favorites, beef and pork, to fish and poultry, the change was so great that the cattle market immediately plummeted.

I began drinking enough water daily to fill a child's

wading pool. When I walked around, I became convinced that I could hear a sloshing sound not unlike an incoming tide.

The water meter for our house began spinning at such an alarming rate that we considered asking the city for an industrial rate.

The path to a perfect body hasn't been all that easy. In fact, the path became strewn with countless obstacles. The first was my personal prediction that, at my earliest weight loss rate, I would reach my goal by the year 2000. The other obstacle occurred on the precise day that I began the Weight Watcher program.

In a cruel twist of fate, that was also the day that I assumed responsibility for chocolate sales for two schools. For two weeks, I counted boxes of chocolate bars and reluctantly turned them over to my high school students. My dilemma would have fit in perfectly with Dante's concept of Inferno.

While my students talked to me with chocolate on their breath and I counted out their allotments of chocolate bars, I became convinced that any weight loss would be a sheer miracle.

A Gift of Chocolates

In good faith, my husband gave me a box of chocolates for Valentine's Day. It was in good faith because everyone in our house knows deep down inside that the day will come when I will wear a size ten again. That's an unspoken fact in our house. We all believe that the sun will  come up every morning, that good triumphs over evil and that I will again wear the size tens which are gathering dust in the back of my closet.

As I opened the heart-shaped box of chocolates on Valentine's Day morning, I silently vowed that I would repay him for his good faith. I would not throw caution to the wind and devour the contents of the candy box like so many handfuls of popcorn. No, I would savor each piece in its own good time and I would, for the first time in my life, exhibit stoic restraint.

As I carefully nibbled on a chocolate-covered nougat, I decided on a plan of action which would demonstrate to all of the world my mature resistance to chocolate. The morning went along well, considering I teach during the mornings at a school thirteen miles from home.

The first thing that I saw upon returning home was the box of chocolates on the kitchen counter. Because I had had a fairly successful morning at school, I decided to reward myself with a chocolate-covered caramel. My great plan was to eat the chocolates as a system of rewards, perhaps extending the longevity of the candy well into the Christmas holiday season. How the members of my family would marvel at my inner strength and determination!

I decided to hide the heart-shaped box out of sight. My only problem was that I kept remembering where I had hidden it. The chocolates were moved to the top of the refrigerator to the freezer to under my bed.

That afternoon I cleaned the oven for the first time in two years, and considering the effort put into that task, I rewarded myself with a chocolate chew followed by a chocolate jelly.

By late afternoon, my plan had deteriorated rapidly. I found myself being rewarded for walking up and down the stairs, watering the houseplants and breathing steadily. In haste I threw away the tell-tale empty candy wrappers and shuffled around the remaining pieces in the box in an attempt to cover up my indiscretions. My trips to the chocolate box became more frequent and considerably less discreet.

At dinnertime, with my digestive system in a state of mild rebellion, I picked at the food on my plate. My family marvelled at my attempt to diminish my intake of both food and chocolates on the same day. Because of guilt feelings over my chocolate-covered ruse, I consoled myself with the rest of the chocolates. By late evening, I related to the character Ray Milland played in "Lost Weekend". The size tens seemed further away then ever.

There is only one thing that puzzles me about chocolate. That's how a person can gain ten pounds by eating only one pound of chocolates. There ought to be a law.

Sweet Revenge

While our children were growing up, we were often warned about the Empty Nest Syndrome by older parents. According to their horror stories, we would suddenly find ourselves bouncing around in an empty house without the warmth and companionship of those extra bodies. Our lives would become shallow and meaningless.

Like Santa Claus and the Tooth Fairy, the Empty Nest Syndrome is more fiction than fact. A U.S. Department of Education report has revealed that more young people, between the ages of 18 and 24, are opting to live with the old folks at home. In 1985, the figure had risen to 53.6 percent and it continues to increase.

Having our children return to the roost doesn't really fit into our long-range plans for the future. In fact, we had looked forward to becoming a burden to our children in our old age, rather than the opposite.

After 25 years of walking through sticky spill marks on our kitchen floor and spending about 10 years of that time turning off lights, it would be nice to turn the tables for once.

We have always encouraged our daughters to live in various parts of the country, in hopes that we could live in their homes on a rotating schedule. We could move out of our present home and live perhaps in the South for the winters and then migrate to the North for the summers.

I'm looking forward to leaving the lights on and staring into an open refrigerator for endless hours in someone else's home. I would like to know what it's like to turn my Perry Como tapes up to full volume and listen to them until the late hours of the night, when people are trying to sleep.

We wouldn't really need a car for transportation

because we could always borrow the girls'. We could cruise from one senior citizen center to another at night and be sure to return at least two hours past the time that we promised to be home. We would never have to buy gas for the car and our children would surely understand if the gas tank was always returned on empty.

The language of a dependent should be easy to learn. I'm sure that we could easily master the most common phrases.

"Did you have a good day?"

"Uh-huh."

"What did you do?"

"Nothing."

We are already practicing the most complicated phrase of all, "What's for dinner?", and we are quite fluent with the correct response, "What? THAT again?"

Final terms about allowances still have to be worked out and are at this point negotiable. We can only hope that our daughters will appropriately reward us if we keep our room neat and help wash the dishes once in a while.

Life in the Slow Lane

With all three of our daughters home for the summer, our family has lost a great deal of its spontaneity.

While they were off at college or attending the local high school, going to town or to the grocery store was a relatively simple affair. In five minutes or less, I could change my clothes, put on my makeup and compose a comprehensive shopping list.

This may not prove to be a scientific theory, but there appears to be a direct relationship between age and the time it takes to get ready to leave the house.

If I tell the girls that I'm leaving for the grocery store in five minutes, my open invitation is met with a chorus of common laments: "But, my hair!", "I'll need 30 minutes!" or "Be with you as soon as I do my face!"

Having learned from previous experiences, I now warn them of my departure time at least one hour in advance. As a matter of fact, I start getting ready when they appear to be finished. During the time between the first warning and our actual departure, there is sufficient time to bake and frost a cake, paint one side of the house or strip and wax the kitchen floor.

As the girls prepare to face the outside world, the bathroom becomes a labyrinth of electrical cords and an arsenal of cosmetics. Electrical cords are connected to hair dryers, hair curlers, face scrubbers and cuticle buffers. Blushers, lipsticks, eye makeup and all of the other

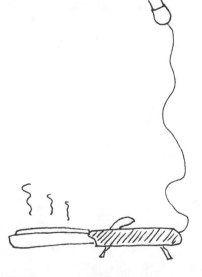

essentials are spread out on every imaginable surface throughout the bathroom. Given their supply of makeup, it would be possible to transform Godzilla into a femme fatale.

While I pace the floor and wonder if the stores will still be open by time we get there, the girls brush, comb, tweeze, blow-dry, powder and manicure. As I nervously eye the clock, they go through enough aloe products to justify another harvest of the plants. In our house, no face will go to town before its time.

It's not that the girls are homely by any stretch of the imagination. Each one has the appropriate number of facial features and they appear in the right order on their faces. Their skin is smooth and taut and they are hardly the stuff of which monster movies are made.

In the time that it takes to hold a SALT conference or to deliver a set of twins, they have managed to straighten all of the curly hair and curl all of the straight hair and they are ready to go.

When they have left the house for the car, I quickly change my clothes, run a comb through my hair and dab on some lipstick. Inevitably, I forget to pick up half of the items on my grocery list, leave my checkbook at home or develop a run in my nylons between the produce section and meat department, but at least the girls look nice.

Allowances

The phone will ring at any moment. If any of our daughters have been reading newspapers, my husband and I will have a lot of explaining to do.

"Mom, did you read the news this week? Most kids get weekly allowances!"

Now that the going rates for children's allowances have made front page news, that phone call is inevitable. I have never felt this way about censorship of the press.

It isn't the violence in the news that concerns me, but rather the unsettling news that the average 16-year-old in this country is raking in an $8.13 weekly allowance. According to the article, most of this money is shelled out for keeping their rooms neat and receiving good report cards from school.

Until this week we ha.' convinced our daughters that twenty-five cents was a reasonable weekly allowance. Under this high-rolling system of finance, it would be possible for them to buy a shoelace at any given time, or for that matter, a pack of gum or a No. 2 pencil. If they chose to save their money, it would be possible to buy a candy bar or some other luxury.

We have operated under the unorthodox theory that clean rooms and good report cards are expected behavior rather than special favors bestowed upon parents. If they needed money for lunch tickets at school or life's little essentials, it was given to them. While they were still young, we discovered that a simple "I'm proud of you" carried as much clout as a dollar bill.

At one point, if I remember correctly, there was a slight skirmish over the topic of allowances. One of our daughters suggested that it might be nice to receive perhaps a $3 weekly allowance for cleaning her room and unloading the dishwasher.

"Fine" I acknowledged. "And I would like to receive an allowance from all of you for washing the clothes, making the meals and keeping the rest of the house in order." I quickly calculated that this allowance would roughly amount to $13,000 per child for each year.

"This is a family that we're talking about, not a union shop", I maintained. "We all do things for each other, without considering how much that job is worth."

The revolution was quelled and the girls eventually found outside jobs to support their lifestyles. After all, we were only talking about 25 cents.

Now that the press has blurbed out the news that the typical allowance is in fact much higher, I fear another insurrection. If they should start talking about retroactive pay and accrued interest, things could get pretty serious. In the case of our oldest daughter, we might have to turn over our house and our collection of records from the sixties. The younger daughters might choose to repossess our cars.

Of course, I could always retaliate with my old sermonette about family responsibilities and present them each with a bill for dishwashing, laundry and parental counseling.

It's a Boy! It's a Girl!

A couple in Louisiana planned the recent birth of a son. As part of the woman's in vitro fertilization, the couple chose to have a boy.

I must admit that I'm adamantly traditional when it comes to choosing the sex of an offspring. I'm also traditional about electric typewriters over word processors and long-cooking rice over the five-minute variety. I wonder if we should mess around with Mother Nature.

I fret about the man-woman ratio in our country becoming out of balance, leaving thousands of girls without prom dates and other devastating consequences.

Having a baby should be a lot like opening a birthday present. The only difference is that you carry the present around for nine months without knowing its contents. It's the source of office pools and friendly wagers.

If lab techniques can allow couples to choose the sexes of their babies, where is the element of surprise?

My husband and I had four such surprises. Because all of our daughters were surprises, we dressed them in boys' clothing. The explanation was simple.

Before the birth of our first daughter, I went to a sale on baby clothing. The baby shop was a madhouse.

About fifty women, all of whom appeared to be smuggling basketballs under their clothing, were engaged in stomach-to-stomach combat over baby toys and clothing.

Amid the shouting and general chaos, I found two snowsuits- one pink, the other blue. Knowing that we would eventually have a boy, I chose the blue.

For ten consecutive years, I had to explain to all concerned that our "little fellows" were indeed girls. In desperation, I resorted to taping bows to their heads. I discovered early in the game that a baby's sex is pretty much perceived by its clothing.

Actually, the only thing that kept me in the delivery room was finding out if we had had a boy or a girl. Other than that element of surprise, deliveries have few pleasures to offer.

If parents decide to determine the sex of their babies, they will be able to shout out "It's a boy!" or "It's a girl!" for months before their babies are born. Gone forever would be the old cliche, "I don't care if it's a boy or a girl, as long as it's healthy".

Another tradition would also fall by the wayside. Instead of offering cigars extolling "It's a girl!" or "It's a boy!", cigars and candy bars handed out by proud fathers would bear the simple inscription, "It's what we expected!"

Answering Machines

Our daughters in college apparently have no shame. They both have answering machines on their telephones.

Gone forever are the days when our daughters could pick up their phones and hear, "This is Mom. Why haven't you been writing home? Blah-blah-blah." With our phone contacts restricted to 30 seconds, I only have time to blurt out, "This is your...(beep)." It's a definite step backward in mother-daughter bonding.

Needless to say, it's somewhat upsetting to pay for a long-distance phone call and to receive a canned message and two beeps. I miss the days when I placed a call to one of their dorms and would hear their voices, live and untaped.

It wouldn't be all that bad, after all, to hear one of them answer in person, "Hi, Mom. I need more money." A taped voice recording is a poor substitute for the real thing.

Emily Post once took the pains to sit down and write eight long pages about proper telephone manners. Judging from what is going on today, she could have much better used her time watching game shows on television or writing chain letters. In a world of party lines and correct greetings, she never reckoned with push-botton machines and taped recordings.

Another disturbing telephone feature is call waiting. This happens during rare, real-life conversations and usually in the middle of one of my more interesting anecdotes. I might be explaining how the city has reversed its garbage collection routes or how cold it is, when I will suddenly hear, "Could you hold? I have another call."

Call waiting is quickly becoming a common annoyance in both business and personal phone calls. What's even worse is having the other party say,

"Could I call you back? I have a long distance call on the other line." If I'm calling long distance, too, I'm tempted to ask, "So what do you think I'm making this call with? A long string and two tin cans?"

In the not too distant past, it was also possible to make a simple phone call to a business without being put on hold and being forced to listen to ten minutes' worth of elevator music.

In spite of my objections to telephone answering machines, I must admit they do have their advantages. Because none of their incoming calls go unnoticed, people no longer will be able to complain about being in the wrong place at the wrong time. An answering machine removes all doubts about missed social invitations and crucial business opportunities.

Although my observations may date me, I miss talking with real people and real telephone operators. Personal contacts have been eliminated by the advances of modern technology and simply pushing a playback button.

The Basement

All winter long, through arctic temperatures and bone-chilling blizzards, we had dreamed of such a moment. There we were, husband and wife, sitting in our lawn chairs surrounded by our children. Above the noises of our daughters and the transistor radio, we could hear the cascading sounds of a waterfall.

We had leisure time on our hands and there was not a mosquito in sight. Only one harsh fact ruined the allusion for us: we were sitting in the basement on a Sunday night. The waterfall was the result of the basement window-well filling to the brim with rain water.

Tornado warnings are a way of life in this part of the country and we have a tendency to forget about them when we pine away for warm summer weather. On this night in particular, a tornado had been spotted three miles southwest of our farm and we decided to retreat to the safety of the basement.

If there is one lesson that we have learned while living on the farm, it's respect for the weather. We have seen our lowly outhouse reduced to splinters in the path of devastating winds and have watched our wooden granary lifted from its concrete base and deposited fifteen feet away in the field. High winds and funnel clouds are humbling experiences.

One thought did occur to me when we headed for the basement for the second time that week. If we should ever have company on such a night, they would be appalled by the appearance of our basement.

The basement of our house is purely functional.

Unlike many basements which are carpeted and paneled, our basement is a somber room enclosed by four concrete block walls. Whenever I go down there, I think of Dostoevski or Edgar Allan Poe.

One whole wall is lined with canning jars and boxes marked "Save". The jars are mostly dill pickles that didn't turn out, feeble attempts at winemaking and some jars which could be suitably labeled "origin unknown". Covered with a thin veneer of dust and an occasional dead cricket, the jars give a mute testimony to the time when we decided to be self-sufficient and live off the land.

Other paraphernalia on the shelves attest to the other stages in our lives: yogurt making and candle making.

While the basement shelves remind us of our past interests, they also tell of our failures. Broken radios, toasters, corn poppers and coffee makers line one shelf in quiet disarray, an ominous salute to the fallibility of man.

The shelves on the remaining walls represent a hodge-podge of our past: a flag with 48 stars, Ford/Dole posters, Christmas ornaments, ice-skates too small for any of us, camping equipment and baseball bats.

The basement serves us as a laundry room, a catch-all for things we can't bear to throw away and as a display room for the grandest collection of cobwebs this side of the Minnesota River. It may never appear on the pages of "Better Homes and Gardens", but it serves its purpose well. It is also a perfect refuge when the spring winds are howling outside.

Refrigerator Cultures

The bread in U.S. Army mess kits will soon have an expected shelf life of three years.

Scientists spent several years developing the long-lasting bread at the U.S. Army's Natick (Mass.) Research Center. The Army could have saved considerable time and dollars on that little project by simply looking into my refrigerator. Some fuzzy, green dishes have been alive there since I was married in 1962.

Not only do those dishes have a shelf life, they also move and grow. Things have gotten so out of hand, that when someone in my family decides to have "a meal on the run", it really happens.

My fascination with mold cultures dates back to my days in grade school, when a teacher instructed us to place a human hair in a dish of jello and then refrigerate it. By the third day, bacteria on the hair would have supposedly developed into an intelligent life form and we were expected to share the scientific results with the students in class.

Unfortunately, my father ate my experiment on the second day. He dashed my ambitions about becoming another Madame Curie by complaining that someone had left a hair in the jello.

I dislike throwing out food. A jar of capers on the back shelf of the refrigerator bears mute testimony to one of the proverbs of my youth: waste not, want not.

The capers date back to the one day that I decided to become a gourmet cook. Since my fascination with exotic dishes only lasted through one meal, the capers simply exist with no useful purpose. They originated near the Mediterranean, and the pickled, green flower buds are used to flavor sauces.

My rationale in keeping them over all these years is that if someone went through all the bother of picking them and shipping them to the states, the least I can do is store them a while longer.

A fine scum has formed on the top of the capers, but it's no worse than the interesting lifeforms appearing on the tops of other containers in the refrigerator.

I can't recall ever taking an oath that I would someday determine what should live and what should die in our refrigerator. When we married, my vows didn't say "I promise to love, cherish and clean out the refrigerator." If someone is that upset with curdled milk, rancid cheese or little packages creeping across the refrigerator shelves, I don't intend to spoil the excitement.

A foods services officer at Canada's National Defense headquarters had a sample of our Army's new bread and noted, "It's very pleasant, almost homemade tasting." Judging by the standards in our home, the bread may taste slightly moldy.

The Battle of the Thermostat

Fast on the heels of the great air conditioner conflict, my husband and I are now experiencing the war of the furnace.

Ours is a mixed marriage. While my husband virtually celebrates the stifling heat of summer and the frigid cold of winter, I prefer to believe that my environment can be controlled with the mere flick of a switch.

With an attitude that is partly patriotic and partly concerned with creature comforts, I would really hate to put all of those furnace and air conditioner people out of work.

Over the years, I have been convinced that my husband should have been born someplace near the Arctic Circle. He could have frolicked with the polar bears in subzero temperatures and watched his breath freeze. On the other hand, he would have been equally at home with the heat in Death Valley.

In the early fall, while the leaves are still clinging to their branches, I have been known to run the furnace in the morning and the air conditioner in the afternoon.

During the entire year, our wall thermostat is in a constant state of motion, as he turns it one way and I turn it another. It has been rotated so many times that most of the numbers have been worn off, which is all right, because I suspect that when my husband looks at it, he only sees dollar signs anyway.

During all of our feuding, I can recall only one time when my husband decided that I had overstepped the line.

It was a typical summer day for this part of the country and I was much younger. After doing the usual, mundane things, like vacuuming, dusting and watching the candles melt, I decided it would be nice to have a fire in the fireplace.

It was only logical that the temperature in the house would have to be reduced to accommodate for a blazing fire, so I illogically turned down the air conditioner as low as it would go.

Imagine my husband's surprise when he returned home from work and walked into a kitchen which resembled a large walk-in cooler. When he called out my name, he no doubt could see his breath.

It would be almost impossible to describe the look in his eyes when he walked into the living room and saw the fire blazing away. It was a look of total disbelief. On the other hand, it could have been the aftereffect of walking through a series of rooms with extreme temperatures.

He didn't get angry. In fact, he said nothing.

"I really missed having a fire," I explained.

He made a funny, groaning noise.

It was almost as if he had figured out what the words, "For better or for worse," finally meant.

The Egg-splosion

Except for the explosion in my kitchen, this has really been a ho-hum week. I never realized that two eggs could do so much damage.

I take that back. When we were first married, I burned a hard-boiled egg, an incredible feat by most standards. I left an egg simmering in a pan of water while I went shopping. While I was gone, the water completely evaporated, the egg blew up and all that was left were charred remains. For several weeks afterwards, our kitchen smelled like a chemistry experiment gone out of control.

I had never killed an egg before.

This week I decided to do something different and special for my husband. I would make him a meal. I thought he might appreciate something that wasn't served on a cardboard circle, covered with cheese and pepperoni, and made him feel Italian.

In order to make his favorite German potato salad, I had to first hard-boil two eggs. When I attempted to peel the eggs, I was dismayed to discover that they were still soft and squishy. No problem. I would finish cooking them in the microwave oven.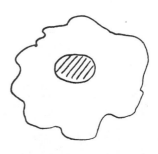

Microwave ovens have a certain mystique. I have no idea how they work or how they can heat hot dogs without warming the plate. Microwave ovens are like word processors and VCRs: the less you know, the better. If I wanted to know how those things work, I would have majored in physics.

After I heated the eggs for a reasonable time in the microwave, I placed the dish on the counter. I had just turned around when there was the resounding noise of an explosion. At first, I thought a car in the street had backfired. The eggs had completely disintegrated.

There were pieces of egg on the ceiling, walls and floor. There were flecks of egg in the toaster, on the window and in my hair. My entire kitchen had turned into an egg dish. All it lacked was a sprig of parsley for garnish.

I gave serious thought to locking the door behind me and running away.

Pieces of egg fell from the ceiling like yellow and white confetti, but I wasn't feeling very jubilant. It was depressing when I realized that I had taken two days' work from some chicken and ruined it in a matter of seconds. Salvaging the eggs seemed out of the question. There were too many foreign, unidentifiable objects in them when I swept the floor.

If so much damage could be done with two little eggs, I dread to think about what could happen to a 24-pound turkey on Thanksgiving.

Festival Hits the Mark

For nearly every town in this part of the country, there appears to be another festival. Whether or not the festivities are set aside to promote a special crop of the area or to promote tourism is beside the point. What is mind-boggling is the fact that for every festival there is a planning committee, made up of interested members of those communities, whose job it is to make the festival unique and memorable.

From the goat races in Jasper to the Strawberry Festival in Afton to the Turkey Races in Worthington to the Dutch Days in Edgerton, each town is determined to make their festival the one outstanding event of the year.

It must be difficult for those committees to come up with interesting ideas for festivals year after year when the tallest building in town is the grain elevator and the citizens are clamoring for a little excitement.

Of all of the festivals which have been touted recently, a small town in south central Minnesota should claim top honors in the creativity department. The town recently held a summer festival which was highlighted by a Bessie the Cow Contest.

In a nutshell, the concept of the contest was pretty basic. A cow was penned up in a square corral, which had been 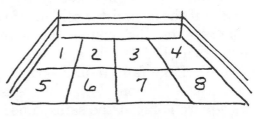 marked off into numbered grids. Prior to the festival, chances on the various numbered squares of the grid were sold by committee members for a nominal fee.

After the crowning of the new festival queen and the other preliminaries, all attention was focused on Bessie the Cow.

No doubt, children with balloons and other spectators with sun-burned faces from standing out long hours in the sweltering sun crowded around the pen and awaited the moment when Bessie would eventually do what came naturally on one of the numbered squares. The person holding the matching number would win the contest and presumably, the cleaning up honors went to someone else.

I wonder what that committee will do next year to top the excitement of the Bessie the Cow Contest. Next year they might be able to double the size of the pen, allowing them to sell more chances and have a bigger prize. Or if someone got really creative, they could substitute Percival the Pig for the cow and be able to use smaller squares.

How about brown t-shirts emblazoned with "I watched Bessie do Her Thing" or "My folks watched Bessie the Cow and all I got was this lousy shirt"? Menus in the local cafes could be specially created for the summer festival and a nice touch would be to have chocolate pie and call it "Bessie the Cow Pie". The list of possibilities seems endless. Let's face it, those folks that thought up the contest have only scratched the surface.

Although I couldn't get away for the contest, I wonder if the committee sold all of their chances and if a picture of the winner appeared in the weekly newspaper. Did Bessie appear to be very concerned with all of the fanfare and hoopla as she became the center of attention? What happens when more than one square is hit at the same time?

Next summer I hope to know some of those answers and I already have a wild hunch about square number eleven.

Golf

I have never been able to operate within certain time guidelines. Although my meal preparations look like a rerun of the old television game show, "Beat the Clock", my two-minute eggs and seven-minute frostings still take half an hour. A twenty-minute coffee cake can land up languishing in my oven for the better part of a morning.

While most human pregnancies last nine months, mine seemed to go on interminably. With these precedents behind me, it's almost a certainty that I would never be able to play on an 18-hole golf course in either Denver or Los Angeles.

The city of Denver has rules governing the length of play on any of its municipal golf courses, and Los Angeles hopes to follow suit. The operators of those city golf courses erroneously assume that a person should be able to play 18 holes of golf in four-and-a-half hours.

That's the equivalent of having 75 strokes per nine holes. Unfortunately for me, 75 happens to be my best bowling score rather than my best golf score.

On the rare occasions that I accompany my husband to a golf course, our usual game will include a beautiful sunrise and a breath-taking sunset. A day at the golf course is exactly what it implies.

As I zig-zag from one side of the fairway to the other, a 330-yard golf hole may mean a three-mile walk. I realize that the shortest distance between two points is a straight line, but in my golf game there is no such thing as a straight line.

Actual hours will pass by as I trudge from golf hole to another, seeking out my errant golf balls and wayward tees. Most of my game is spent on my knees, as I try to locate my golf balls from under bushes, in long grass, in waterways and in roadside ditches.

The Los Angeles plan would set a time limit of two hours and 20 minutes for the first nine holes of golf, according to a recent news release. Park rangers would be stationed at the 10th tee and could ask any foursome that exceeds the limit to leave the course. Course marshals would patrol the fairways, encouraging laggards to hurry up.

If our local golf courses were to follow the examples set by these larger cities, my golf game would become more nerve-wracking than it already is. If I knew that some sort of bouncer was about to oust me from the course at any moment, I would become a neurotic mess.

I would actually have to run around the course as I would pursue my golf ball from one landing spot to the next. In addition to the running, I would have to carry my golf club bag, which is usually packed with clubs, extra balls, all of my makeup, several cans of pop and a day's supply of sandwiches.

Given these conditions, it might be much easier and much less stressful for me to go through basic training in the Army or to take up mountain climbing.

Putting the Byte into Computers

They are in our midst. They have managed to squeeze their way into almost every corner of our lives. They have appeared in our grocery stores, our department stores, our school, our homes, and yes, even our churches.

They are the computers and there is no stopping them. They have even managed to invade one of my favorite reading selections, the classified ads.

This week I came across an ad which read, "We are a multi-processing DOS/VSE shop currently migrating to MVS/XA. Our current environment consists of an IBM 3083, 4341 and 30 S/1's. A major S/1 development effort is being planned."

The invasion appears to be complete. What has happened to the classified ads for teachers, nurses and custodians? Most important of all, what is a DOS/VSE? Have I received the vaccinations for it? Without knowing more, I am sure that I would never allow one of our daughters to date one.

As the result of a culture which gave us "Ozzie and Harriet", the hoola-hoop, and hi-fi record players, I am not ready to accept the challenge of the computers. I was meant for a much simpler life. My electric typewriter and electric can-opener are about as technical as I hope to get.

It took me eight years to master Spanish classes, and it's doubtful whether I could handle another language. If a person with whom I am talking begins to ramble on about floppy discs, bytes, programs or interfacing, my mind begins to wander. If they should hit upon REM's, Cobals, and print-outs, I feel feverish and begin to hallucinate.

It wasn't all that long ago when software kept our leftovers fresh in the refrigerator and memory was the ability to remember birthdays and anniversaries. Interfacing had something to do with sewing and hardware meant hammers, nails and buckets of paint. Print-outs were what you resorted to before you learned cursive writing and keyboards were musical instruments.

Gathering from what I do understand about the subject, I should be able to do my meal-planning, household budgeting and cross-filing of cooking recipes for a price roughly in the neighborhood of $1500. If I had $1500 to spend, I would most likely give up cooking anyway, and wouldn't need the system.

I have discovered through conversations with my colleagues at work that my anti-computer notions border on un-Americanism. It's like taking a swipe at Mom, apple pie or the flag. As a member of a minority in a world convinced about the benefits of computers, I have until this time closeted my misgivings about floppy discs and talking to machines.

If my recipes turn out to be dismal failures or my checkbook fails to balance, I will only have myself to blame.

Moby Perch

Challenges come to us in many forms. To some people, a challenge may mean climbing to the summit of a mountain, winning a marathon or mastering some obscure language.

My moment of triumph came this week when I baited a fish hook for the very first time. For years I have been telling friends how much I enjoy fishing, yet I had never baited a hook, touched a live fish or cleaned a fish for cooking. My idea of fishing was to sit on the end of the dock and to yell for help whenever a fish took the line. I was hardly Izaak Walton material.

Until this past week there were several other things that I would rather have done than grab a wriggling nightcrawler or a slippery minnow and impale it on a shiny hook. For instance, I would have preferred to have root canal surgery or have a speeding violation listed in the local newspaper.

My husband and I had been fishing for several hours one day when I announced, "I would like to bait a hook". It was one of those crazy inspirations which proved to be irreversible. Once the words were spoken there was no going back, and it reminded me of the times that I have suggested, "Let's have another baby".

With a bare fishhook in hand, I pulled the minnow bucket out of the water. Catching a minnow in a bucket is not as easy as it looks. As the slippery, elusive minnows swam through my fingers, the challenge was formidable. Keeping a hold on a minnow once it is caught is even more difficult.

"What do I do now?" I asked my husband, who was observing the process with stifled laughter.

"Put the hook in right behind his dorsal fin, so that it will look like he's swimming in the water". Dorsal fin, right. Knowing nothing about the anatomy of a fish, I could have easily located the minnow's appendix. I tried to avoid the minnow's glassy stare as I plunged the hook through its flesh and inbedded the barb of the hook in my right thumb.

This experience might seem inconsequential to any seasoned fisherman, but for me it was a sheer victory. For a fleeting moment, I felt as though there were nothing that I couldn't do. I had actually baited a hook.

Once the hook was lowered in the water, my problems multiplied. The bait succeeded in attracting a four-inch perch. I was caught up in the spirit of the moment and cried out, "I'll take if off!" If it had been a bullhead, I probably would not have been as brave.

Out of fear of touching the fish, I held onto it tightly with the bottom of my shirt. For what seemed like endless hours, I wrestled with the swallowed hook. I grimaced and tried talking to the fish as the hook was wiggled this way and that. Just as I was about to call the operation a complete failure, the hook worked free along with some portions of the fish which were apparently unnecessary.

The fish was returned to the water and swam away. To this day he is probably relating his tale of his inadvertent tonsillectomy. I have no desire to bait another hook. Once that first mountain is conquered, what else is there?

The Sunglasses

I may not have a telephone booth, where I change into a caped crusader, but I do make a dramatic transformation five days a week. My dual personality comes into focus when I make the transition from being an English and Spanish teacher in one school system during the mornings and then travel 12 miles to another school, where I teach Spanish during the afternoons. To paraphrase the old television series, "Paladin", I have books- will travel.

Now that spring has arrived, and the threat of swerving into a ditch or getting stuck in some remote snowbank has been drastically minimized, I have discovered that I truly enjoy those rides between the two schools. For one-half hour every weekday, I munch merrily away on my tuna fish sandwich and my imagination takes over.

As soon as I get into my car and shut the door, I am no longer a mild-mannered teacher, intent on setting the world right about double negatives and split infinitives.

As the rural landscape rushes by, I am Isadora Duncan, the famous ballerina, sitting behind the wheel of her sports car. I am a Daytona race car driver, taking the curves with the greatest of ease and with the crowds rising to their feet, wild with frenzy. I am the moll who drives the robbery getaway car, with my car trunk full of stolen millions and the police hot on my trail.

On one sunny noon this past week, I escaped to my car at the designated hour for another rendezvous with destiny. Because the sun was so bright that day, I slipped on my oversized sunglasses, which I personally feel make me look like a cross between Sophia Loren and Jacqueline Onassis.

By the time I had driven halfway between my two

schools, I had met several people I knew, driving their pickups and cars in the opposite direction. I waved to them and they waved back. I could see their smiles as they passed by. They almost appeared to be laughing.

One small detail kept bothering me, however. The sun was so bright and strong that I had to keep on squinting in order to see the road. I drove another mile or two before I happened to glance into the rearview mirror. One of my lenses was missing.

In that one moment of truth, I could understand why the people I had met on the road has smiled so much when I waved at them. Rather than resembling a gang moll, Isadora Duncan or some other romantic personality, I bore a strong resemblance to a one-eyed racoon.

That little escapade certainly didn't do much for my image. Until I locate that missing lens, my noontime adventures will have to be put on hold.

The Septic Tank

I don't miss our old septic tank. Now that we have moved back to town, I sleep better at nights, knowing that our house is magically connected to an up-to-date sewer system, which is supervised by people trained in that field.

It is comforting to know that miles of pipes and plumbing stand between us and the possibility of a septic tank backup.

For nearly fourteen years, our happiness was dictated by a malevolent monster which was contructed of concrete, tiles and a drain field. After our first unpleasant encounters with the septic tank we were convinced that it had a personality of its own. Like someone's description of flying, there were days of boredom interrupted by moments of sheer terror.

The tank loathed any kind of work. If there were showers to be taken or clothes to be washed, it would moan and groan and reluctantly begin to work. The more we coaxed, cajoled and plunged the system, the more belligerent it would become.

I followed other people's advice and regularly fed the monster seemingly lethal doses of chemicals and baker's yeast, hoping to elicit some favorable response. The results always seemed short-lived, however, and we would soon find ourselves in hipboots, trying to retrieve our belongings from the basement, which more often than not resembled an indoor swimming pool.

It despised company of any sort. In terms of personality, our septic tank was definitely a loner. If we unwisely chose to host a family dinner during the holidays or a graduation reception, the tank would sulk, pout and finally refuse to do any work at all.

There are few things more depressing than to have a nice table set, the dinner about to come out of the oven and then to have some city guest lift his nose and ask, "What is that dreadful smell?" Any reference to a faulty septic tank at a time like that has a tendency to squelch the healthiest of palates. It's difficult to appreciate a good meal when you know that one floor below the dining room table Mount Vesuvius is about to erupt and spoil all of the fun.

Nor are city guests, fresh from the lap of luxury and an antiseptic sewer system likely to respond favorably to the whispered warning, "Don't flush!" Unless they have had first-hand experience with seeing a basement turn into a Black Hole of Calcutta, they will never understand. When dinner guests see the farm neighbor's honey wagon back up to the septic tank to undo the damage, roast beef just doesn't taste the same.

There is a code of honor among country dwellers which includes not mentioning the other person's septic tank, unless of course, that person wants to bring up the topic. If neighbors walked into our farmhouse and were enveloped in a cloud of sewer gas, they would act as if nothing had happened. Judging from their nonresponse, it could have been a whiff of Chanel No. 5.

Now that the monster is someone else's concern, I feel much more confident.

Remote Control Blues

Move over, Shirley MacLaine. I think I am having out-of-body experiences. I don't have to travel in another dimension to Tibet, ancient Egypt or some other exotic place, either. All I have to do is sit in our living room and watch cable television with my husband.

Before we moved into town and the cable TV was installed like some giant umbilical cord into our living room, life was relatively simple. We had three or four channels on which to base our entertainment. Because of my husband's innate fear that there might be something more interesting on another channel, I had become used to watching three or four programs at a time. I could handle that.

Suddenly we have been introduced to the marvelous options of 27 television stations. No longer content to watch four television programs during the same hour, my husband uses the remote control as if it were a joy stick for a video game.

During any evening, my husband can be found clicking buttons as if there were no tomorrow, and heaven forbid, no reruns. One hour of prime time can give us countless murders, ball games, espionage plots and sit-coms. By simply blinking my eyes, it is possible for me to miss two or three shows.

Before the event of cable television in our lives, it was possible to watch most programs from beginning to end. We were content to watch film credits and commercials between our favorite programs. As a result of television overlapping, we have been making less runs to the refrigerator for late night snacks. If our remains should be discovered someday, reduced to nothing but skin and bones, let it be known that our cable television is at fault.

The only exception to our madcap television viewing was this past week when the World Series was televised. The remote control literally gathered dust during all of the games. For those precious few days, one station stayed on the screen at all times and even the commercials captured our undivided attention. That's pretty amazing considering that before the series began, I didn't know the difference between a Blyleven and a bagel.

Now that the series is over, our set has once again become a living kaleidoscope of sights and sounds. No sooner have the doctors on "St. Elsewhere" diagnosed a fatal illness, than "Magnum, P.I." has captured a villain on the beach at Maui. We are back to watching seven or eight newscasts at the same time. I have seen the cast members of "M*A*S*H" infiltrate a 1950's movie featuring Jimmy Stewart.

Scripts and plots have again become hopelessly entangled. Johnny Carson speaks with the voice of Dan Rather. As the scenes flip by in rapid succession on the screen, I can only hope that my husband will someday misplace the remote control.

Blood Tests are in Vein

Sociologists may someday support my thesis concerning the rise and fall of the American marriage. I believe that the increase in unsuccessful marriages occured some time after states began dropping the requirements for blood tests before marriage.

At the time of our marriage, which our children believe was sometime during the age of dinosaurs, blood tests were required in the state of Michigan. Now, don't misunderstand me. I would have done almost anything for the man I intended to marry. I would have gladly given up a throne, walked through fire or I would have professed my love in a thousand different ways.

However, when I found out that the fine print in the wedding license specified some blood-letting in the process, I did experience some misgivings. I'm fairly squeamish about blood tests of any kind.

Incidentally, there were two professions open to young women at that time. One was nursing and the other was teaching. Because I faint at the sight of blood, especially mine, I chose teaching.

My fiance had to literally drag me to the doctor's office for the blood tests. The nurse in charge was a no-nonsense type of person with the charisma and physique of an Army sergeant. After she had siphoned off enough of my husband-to-be's corpuscles to fill what resembled a pint jar, she turned to me.

I am not exaggerating when I say the needle she held resembled a javelin, or at least a lethal weapon. When she observed that I was not going to willingly part with any of my blood, she became frighteningly aggressive. In my mind's eye she became a cross between an Amazonian huntress and Lizzie Borden.

"Okay, honey, roll up your sleeve," she barked out. I was quick to respond and within seconds, she had applied a tourniquet to my arm and was searching for the right vein. I might mention here that I don't have veins. At least I don' have any close to the surface of my skin. They are so difficult to find that I have known hematologists who have gone back to school and changed their specialties. My veins have been the subject of awe and dismay in medical centers scattered throughout the Upper Midwest.

The sergeant, after kneading my arm as if it were bread dough, and for what seemed like hours, finally plunged the needle into my arm. Either she or I let out a blood-curdling scream, although in the confusion I couldn't be sure who it was. She dug around futilely, and then she tried again. Beads of perspiration formed on her forehead and my life was passing before my eyes.

She finally sent me home and told me to come back the next day when the doctor would be in the office. That night I thought quite a bit about marriage, the pending blood test and life in general. Marriage isn't quite as romantic a notion when there's an ounce of blood involved. Washing another person's socks is one thing, but becoming a walking blood bank is another.

Fortunately, the doctor produced a gusher the next morning. Otherwise I would be doing quite a lot of explaining to our children and this letter would be written under my maiden name.

Pets are Forever

According to a recent Associated Press news release, there's a new option for pet owners. A company called Preserv-A-Pet in Nisswa, MN, will preserve the remains of departed pets by freeze-drying them.

Pets no longer have to be planted in shoe boxes under backyard trees. With freeze-drying, they may be converted into door stops or conversation pieces in our living rooms.

Outside of the price, there is one catch which I feel obligated to reveal: pet owners must ship their deceased pets to the company frozen. Once the animal arrives in Nisswa, it is thawed and shaped into a lifelike position. It is then freeze-dryed until (Voila!) it becomes a form of instant pet.

Now, in Minnesota this isn't an insurmountable problem for about two-thirds of the year. If a cat, for example, should go to that great litter box in the sky any time between October and April, freezing its remains and sending it through the mail in a frozen condition is an easy task.

But what happens if your canary should go feet up during the summer, or your dog should pick the hottest day of the year to go to its final reward? Let's face it. Under those conditions, there is only one answer: the kitchen freezer.

I must admit that it would be a real challenge to live a normal life, knowing that Lassie, our faithful watchdog, or one of our farm cats was reposing in the refrigerator's freezer.

I would need to know more before I could pursue such a plan. Should the pet be placed in a plastic garbage bag first, or should it be draped over the contents of the freezer, like some departed head of state?

Would it be some form of sacrilege to place the pet near last summer's string beans, or would some other section of the freezer be more appropriate? Personally, I wouldn't like to see a departed pet any place near the ice cream, the unbaked frozen pies or anything else that might be in our freezer.

For one thing, our freezer already contains enough unmarked, mystery packages. On many occasions I have thawed out what I believed to be ground beef and it turned out to be something else. When it comes to our freezer, truth in packaging laws do not apply.

When people go to their freezers for ice-cubes, do they instinctively give Rex or Puff an affectionate pat? How do they explain the contents of the freezer to unsuspecting guests in their homes?

Perhaps the most questionable aspect of this freeze-drying business is where it will all lead. Will it someday amount to some sort of curse to be someone's favorite teacher or beloved relative?

To roughly paraphrase Patrick Henry, I know not which course others may take, but I would prefer not to be a hat rack in someone's living room.

The Russians and the Checks

Residents of Russia will soon be writing checks for the first time.  Their kopecks and rubles will be replaced by checkbooks, my favorite form of creative writing.

The Soviet trade-union newspaper *Trud* reflected the curiosity Soviet citizens feel about the Western convenience when it will be introduced by state banks in December. The newspaper asked, "We have read about them, seen them in foreign movies, but what are they and how do we use them?"

These are good questions and they deserve answers from an expert. When it comes to checkwriting, I wrote the book. Or rather, I didn't write in the book, and as a result, I received my complete education on the subject.

My parents never wrote checks. To this day, my mother pays for things in cash or she sends money orders. Her life has been untouched by overdrafts, monthly statements or unrecorded checks.

I was still a newlywed when I received my first checkbook, with the simple instructions, "Pay the bills." From that point on, things went progressively downhill. When I absent-mindedly signed my maiden name of the first checks, the small Iowa bank simply overreacted. Through a series of curt phone messages, and veiled threats on my life, they made quite clear how they felt about checks with strange names on them.

For the first several years, I completely disregarded bank statements. I treated them as though they were some sort of junk mail from the bank, and never once suspected that they contained debit notices about checking charges and check printing charges. It had somehow never occured to me that we might be charged for using our own money. That mind-boggling notion was brought to my attention through other phone calls from the bank.

As the years passed by, I entered a stage of creative bookkeeping. I began writing checks without recording them, thinking I would write them down once I got home. As a result, I began transposing numbers and a check written at the grocery store for $32 would become $23 once it was duly recorded.

Given my ineptitude for numbers, my checkwriting experiences were doomed from the onset. Rounding off numbers is not an acceptable practice in the world of high finance, and it causes spouses and bankers to run for their Rolaids.

For many Russians, writing checks may prove to be more exciting than sending the first dog into space. I only hope that their bank penalties will not be too steep. Fortunately, my outraged bankers have never given much thought to Siberia.

Chocolate is Good for your Teeth

Some news seems almost too good to be true. A researcher at the University of Texas Health Center in San Antonio says preliminary research suggests that chocolate, or cocoa, the product it comes from, may be a cavity fighter. Tannin, an acidic substance found in cocoa leaves, may be the reason why.

I latched onto that interesting piece of information faster than I can grab up a special of four candy bars for a dollar. I would like to believe that it's true. If chocolate prevents cavities, my teeth should last for a few centuries. My body has undoubltedly become a veritable warehouse for tannin. Over the years I have eaten so much chocolate my blood has turned brown.

Eating chocolate for the sake of my teeth sounds very noble. If some researcher should report that whipping cream is good for some other part of my body, my life would be complete. It would certainly relieve much of my guilt and anxiety.

I decided to share the good news with my dentist and I expected to receive his approval. He takes his work and all dental research pretty seriously. In fact, he is so intent about his profession that he thinks the hymn,

"Crown Him with Many Crowns", is a song about dentistry.

While he was examining my teeth this week, I decided to run the idea past him. I figured that if I could convince this man about the virtues of chocolate, I would go out and buy tons of the stuff after my appointment.

"I justh readth that thocolate ith good for your teeth", I lisped. It was difficult to sound convincing when all ten of his fingers and half of his dental appliances were crammed into my mouth.

He seemed unimpressed with my newly acquired knowledge of dentistry and cavity prevention. After he gave a what-do-you-know-about-it laugh, he replied, "It could be, but you would have to rinse out your mouth with lye afterwards." My dentist also has a droll sense of humor.

I tried to consider my source. Here is a man who spends most of his waking hours extolling the virtues of flossing, using tartar-control toothpaste and the importance of soft bristles. Because he is so busy thinking about those things, he has very little time for anything else.

My dreams of eating chocolate for the health of my teeth were quickly diminished. I also discovered that some people are terribly reluctant to accept new ideas. Why, it wouldn't surprise me to learn that my dentist has never experienced a chocolate craving.

Until this great debate is resolved between the researcher in Texas and my dentist in Minnesota, I will continue eating chocolate.

The Tag Inspector

One of my greatest fears in life has its own scenario. The nightmare begins innocently enough. I am performing one of the glamorous chores that makes up homemaking, such as cleaning the bathroom or looking for socks under a bed. I'm home alone when there's a knock at the kitchen door. I know that it's at the kitchen door because no one uses a front door in the country.

"Who is it?" I shout at the door, while throwing the vacuum cleaner into the closet.

"Agents, ma'am. Tag agents," is the determined reply.

As I open the door, two men wearing trench coats and pulled-down hats and looking very much like Humphrey Bogart flash their badges of identification and brush past me into the kitchen.

"What do you want?" I ask unexpectantly. After having two women's quotas of children, I never want to appear expectant.

"We're here to check the tags, ma'am," answers the meanest looking man. "You know, the tags on the mattresses and furniture."

"Tags?" I reply, rushing past them and shutting the bathroom door so they won't catch a glimpse of the toothpaste splatters on the bathroom mirrors.

"Yes ma'am. You are aware of the law. Each item is tagged 'Do not removed under penalty of law'."

After a thorough search of the house and its contents, the two men return to the kitchen.

"You've done a fine job, ma'am," states the meanest looking one's partner. "We've checked all of the mattresses and the cushions on the chairs and sofas."

I breathe a silent sigh of relief and experience a sense of accomplishment that closely parallels the feeling after finally opening a child-proof cap on a bottle.

Their hats appear to be permanently stuck to their heads. The meanest looking one gives a poor imitation of a smile and says out of the corner of his mouth, "You know, ma'am, it's people like you that make this country great. You'd be surprised how many people bring those mattresses and cushions home from the store and rip those tags right off. You're a credit to your country, ma'am."

Slightly shaken by this surprise search, I explain to my two guests that I have inherited the trait from my mother. Mother also refused to remove the cellophane paper from new lamp shades for fear of being caught.

The nightmare usually ends at this point. I don't care to imagine what the penalty could be, but I would never touch one of those tags.

It's the Tooth

If our family dentist is ever treated for occupational stress, I will be largely to blame. Perhaps, when my mother was expecting me, she was unnerved by a riveter, a jackhammerer or a man wearing a white jacket. Whatever the cause, my greatest fear in life is going to the dentist.

I know people who can say "I'm going to the dentist" in the same manner in which they would say "We're having beans for dinner tonight" or "I will take the trash outside." Going to the dentist for them, and millions of others like them, is merely an appointment on a calendar, a routine chore that must be done.

On a fear scale, my attitude toward going to the dentist rivals that of Marie Antoinette as she faced the guillotine. I have such a low pain threshhold that having my teeth cleaned requires an anesthetic. My yearly checkup is so traumatic that I usually talk about it, or think about it, all year long.

I receive little sympathy from my own family. They are all stoic about going to the dentist and view my fears as some sort of genetic weakness. They pooh-pooh the idea of novocaine, stating it makes them feel worse, and they make small jokes about my fears at my expense.

In hopes of allaying my fears before one of my dental appointments, my husband offered, "It's only 20 minutes. What could possibly happen to you in only 20 minutes?" What could happen? Plenty. Most natural disasters, like hail, earthquakes and fire, need less than 20 minutes to create their havoc. I have given birth in less than 20 minutes. Twenty minutes can seem like a lifetime, given your surroundings.

In all fairness, I must admit that our dentist and his staff try their best to alleviate my fears. Dentistry, in general, has come a long way since patients had to succumb to gas masks and foot-driven drills.

Perhaps the best anecdote about my particular fear of dentists occurred while we were living in Duluth, 22 years ago. After an interminably long time in the dentist's waiting room, which had been spent leafing through a 1943 Collier's Magazine and counting some anxious moments, I was finally summoned to "The Chair" in the next room. Deciding that the time was appropriate for some final last words, I declared, "I would rather have a baby than have my teeth worked on."

The dentist, who had both the quickest wit and quickest drill south of the Iron Range, looked me right in the eye and answered, "Well, make up your mind before I adjust the chair."

Flannel Nighties

A reader of this column writes, "I was wondering if you'd like to create a new wardrobe line. Something is needed for those of us who are less shapely, live in southwest Minnesota and require warmth while sleeping. I've never seen anything very seductive in flannel."

As an avid fan of hot fudge sundaes and chocolate chips, I know all too well that it's impossible to look seductive in any clothing, no matter how high the price tag.

When tent dresses came on the scene several years ago, I thought my prayers had been answered. With tent dresses, there were no waistbands to cut off your circulation and leave you gasping for air. When the roomy dresses became fashionable, I would have bent down and kissed the ground if it would have been physically possible. At the time it was difficult enough to simply look down and see my feet.

The person who invented tent dresses should be revered as a national hero or at least be canonized someday.

Tent dresses lost their appeal when anorexic women complained that the dresses made them look pregnant. So, what's so wrong with looking pregnant? I would much rather look pregnant than fat.

Roomy, flannel nightgowns seem to have acquired the same social stigma. I began wearing flannel nightgowns several years ago. When faced with the choice of looking seductive or not freezing to death, I chose the latter. However, while I'm lounging around the house in my eight voluminous yards of flameproof flannel, I am aware that any similarity between Miss Universe and me is purely coincidental.

This winter I went one step further in my quest for a frost-free body. I bought some flannel sheets. I have since discovered that it is virtually impossible to move when one flannel nightgown is sandwiched between two flannel sheets. The surfaces cling together like strips of velcro.

If I do manage to roll over in my sleep, my nightgown stays in its original position. If I roll over several times, it feels like I'm wearing a straight-jacket. I'm not surprised some mornings to find myself in some impossible yoga contortions.

If I am ever found some morning with my leg wrapped around my throat, my fixation with flannel would be to blame.

I sometimes fantasize about wearing a slinky nightgown and sleeping between satin sheets. I would be cold, but I would look seductive and very thin. The nice thing about fantasies is that you can be any weight you want to be.

Actually, with a slinky nightgown stretched over my present frame, I might resemble the large shiny ball which heralds the New Year in New York City. Given the additional hazard of satin sheets, I would probably keep sliding out of bed all night.

The Dangers of Going Strapless

Strapless dresses are making a comeback. Across the country, countless young women, hoping to defy the laws of gravity, are showing up for proms in strapless dresses.

A recent sewing column headline in the *Des Moines Register* proclaimed, "Young girls sometimes lack the shape to wear a strapless prom dress".

Tell me something new, Des Moines. While the article may not have been as newsworthy as glasnost or the greenhouse effect, it brought back some bittersweet memories of my first and only experience with a strapless dress.

Rather than buy a prom dress for the senior prom in high school, I decided to borrow a dress from one of my girlfriends. It was hot pink, it was strapless and I simply had to wear it. As I put the dress on and got ready for the dance, I never suspected that I was about to have one of the most tortuous evenings of my life and that my arms and shoulders would ache for at least one week afterwards.

To put it delicately, my friend was very buxom, and the dress had been perfect for her. I had given very little thought to our comparative dimensions. In fact, at that time, I had the same chest measurements as my 12-year-old brother.

My biggest problem seemed to be that there was too much dress and not enough of me. It didn't help matters at all when my mother suggested that I compensate for the difference with some wadded tissue or nylon stockings.

Instead, I decided to spend the entire evning with my arms riveted to my sides, in an effort to keep the dress top in place. When I moved, I resembled a robot. While my friends flailed their arms and legs around on the dance floor, I walked around as if the top half of my body had succumbed to some exotic paralysis.

I couldn't dance. I couldn't wave. I couldn't adjust my $10 bouffant hairdo. While the night was still young, my rigid arms and upper torso had extended to a stiff neck.

While my friends had the apparent time of their lives, I lived in dire fear that the slightest move would reveal more to the dance floor than my physical education teacher had seen all year in the girls' locker room. I had no intention of being the first student in the school's history to be expelled for indecent exposure.

If this were fiction, I would mention at this point that things have changed over the years and wearing a strapless dress is no longer a problem. Unfortunately, before I wear a strapless dress again, I will still need suspenders.

Until someone comes up with a better solution than wadded tissue or nylons, I won't be able to appear strapless in public.

The Christmas Tree

Someone else may call it a problem with spatial relationships. I call it the Annual Christmas Tree Debate.

For years I have con-
tinued to defy all laws
of common sense when
it comes to the selec-
tion of a Christmas
tree. Early each
December, we drive
over to the nearest
nursery to "ooh" and
"ah" over the gala
assortment of trees
and wreaths.

There's something
terribly extravagant
about buying a tree which has been hacked down in its prime, displaying it for two weeks in the living room and then throwing it away.

However, we do enjoy this type of wasteful opulence only once a year, so it can't be all bad. It's not as though we wear coats made from endangered species to meetings of the Sierra Club.

My biggest problem with buying a Christmas tree is not guilt, but rather selecting the right size. My husband holds fast to the theory that a Christmas tree, once brought inside a warm house, will double its normal size. He pictures it as a loaf of homemade bread rising out of control or something equally menacing.

On the other hand, I have insisted that a ten-foot tree, even when placed in a stand, will fit perfectly in our living room. It's beside the point that our house has eight-foot ceilings.

As a result of my fetish for tall, stately trees, my husband has had to haul the cumbersome brutes down into the basement and shorten them with a chain saw.

After alterations have been made dealing with the tree's height, there are further adjustments to be made. For the sake of the tree, the piano has to be moved, along with two bulky armchairs, the dining room table and chairs and one supporting wall.

Once the gargantuan tree has taken over the living room, our house begins to resemble the set of a grade-B horror movie. "Invasion of the Body Snatchers" has few scenes to match the horror of watching a Christmas tree as it takes over a good half of a house. Loaded down with our favorite tree decorations and other festoonings, our tree this year appeared to emit an audible sight of relief as it adjusted to the comfortable indoor temperature.

As I write this letter, it stands behind me ominously, leaning its branches on the bookshelves and whatever else it can reach.

I'll be the first to admit that when it comes to buying Christmas trees, my eyes tend to be larger than our living room.

Modern Music

It's easy for me to look back at the 1950's and think about those times as the good old days. In a way, they were. My mother dressed like Harriet Nelson, she used to cook and our clothes always smelled clothesline fresh.

I tend to forget that it was also a time when kids had more cavities and clothes needed ironing. We also had frizzy hair from home permanents long before it became the rage.

More than anything, I miss the vocalists of the past. For those of you too young to remember, it was a time when men had deep, resonant voices and women had high voices. Recordings have become so complicated today that young people simply don't know when to swoon anymore.

When my friends and I used to listen to Clyde McPhatter, Elvis Presley and Fats Domino, there was no doubt in our minds that we were listening to male singers. The same held true when my mother once listened to Frank Sinatra and Bing Crosby.

Last week, while I was spending some time with our daughters, the song, "Fast Car", was playing on the radio. It's a catchy little song with the phrase, "I have a fast car", repeated every three or four seconds.

I innocently reflected, "He has a pleasant voice." It wasn't as if I was making a declaration of war or making a profound statement about the condition of the world. I was just commenting on the general effects of the music.

"HE?" responded one of our daughters. "He? He? That's a SHE, Mom!"

Judging from her concontrolled gales of laughter, I had just made the faux pas of all time. She gave me one of those looks which I have been receiving all to frequently from my students and my daughters. The look said, "Get out of the Stone Age, will you?"

My confusion is honest. Since then I have made a conscientious attempt to listen to popular songs on the radio, and while the music is playing, I guess whether the singer is male or female. I then listen as the disc jockey announces the name of the song and the performer. If I had been correct, Michael Jackson, Prince and the Pet Shop Boys would all be women; Cher and Tracy Chapman would be men. My guesses have been dismal failures.

If recording companies think that most of us like to listen to male singers, who sound as if someone ran their jeans through a dryer set on "high", I guess they know what they're doing. However, I would have dreaded hearing "White Christmas" sung by Bing Crosby in a high falsetto voice. If Elvis would have sung "Heartbreak Hotel" a few octaves higher, even the Army would have rejected him.

When I get worked up about a singer who swears that he loves me, it's very disturbing to discover that he's a she. It's somewhat disconcerting, after 45 years, to discover that I can no longer tell the difference between boys and girls. My high school health class never prepared me for the popular music of today.

Throwing in the Towel

Like so many other mothers, mine has a memory like a steel trap. She may not remember the ages of her children, when World War II ended, or other trivia, but she does have a particular fondness for remembering in exact detail some events that her children would rather forget.

She called from Michigan last week to tell me how my brother, a struggling young artist in Baltimore, keeps losing his bicycles. Actually, three of his bicycles have been stolen, but in Mother's mind, having something stolen and losing something are the same thing.

I immediately disliked the direction the conversation was taking. I was certain that in a matter of minutes she would be talking about the infamous beach towel scandal of 1955. My fears became a self-fulfilled prophecy.

"Remember when you lost your beach towel in sixth grade?" she asked. "Are you still losing things?"

The year I lost my beach towel was the same year that I won the sixth grade spelling contest over the local radio station. The prize had been a five-dollar savings account at the bank. How could I forget? My mother brings up the beach towel incident every ten years.

When I originally told my mother about my mishap with the beach towel, my nest egg for the future had collected interest and was worth about $5.08. I hated breaking the news to Mother because, like so many feudal kings before her, she had a tendency to kill the messenger.

In a speech which lasted so long that a senate filibuster would pale by comparison, Mother ranted and raved about responsibility and she somehow tied in the Great Depression. She talked about walking eight miles to school and there was no stopping her. She was on a roll.

Once she had finished her spiel, the punishment was sure and swift. Without taking time to remove her apron, she grabbed me by the scruff of my neck and drove me down to the local bank. The interior of the bank resembled a cathedral with its marble columns and marble floor. The comparison seemed quite natural in light of the fact that I was feeling like the most penitent of sinners.

Adding injury to insult, my mother proceeded to tell the bank clerk of my wrong doing. She did the same with the sales clerk in the dry goods store next door, where my money earned for spelling P-R-I-V-I-L-E-G-E and L-I-E-U-T-E-N-A-N-T was exchanged for another beach towel.

My mother's repeated question over the phone brought me back to the present "I said, 'Are you still losing things?'"

"No, Mom," I lied. I didn't have the heart to tell her about the groceries left behind at checkout counters, the lost car keys and library books, and the time I left one of the girls behind in a store and drove home without her.

Confession isn't necessarily good for the soul when you're talking with a mother with an iron-clad memory.

Car Wash Blues

While I was in the local car wash this week, I became a firm believer in the adage, "The grass is always greener on the other side of the fence". It became apparent that the water always flows more freely in the next car wash stall.

Our tan car needed a washing for two obvious reasons. One was that someone had thoughtlessly scrawled on the side of the door "Wash me- 1976". The other reason was that the car I was driving was really red, but it only appeared to be tan because of a thick accumulation of road grime.

Only one other stall was occupied when I drove my car into the car wash building. An older woman was busy hosing down her car with one of those powerful jet-spray devices.

At the time I had four quarters to my name. The only other contents of my change purse were a grocery store coupon, which I noticed had expired shortly after I was married, a small clump of lint and a leftover toothpick. I wasn't concerned because the car was small and surely four quarters would allow enough time for a quick wash and rinse.

I grabbed a firm hold of the washer wand and deposited the coins into the appropriate slot in the machine. While the woman in the next stall was holding onto her powerful jet spray hose with both of her hands and the water pressure was virtually catapulting her from one side of the stall to another, my hose only produced a mere trickle.

"How typical", I thought to myself. "I've just dropped my last coins into this crazy machine and it doesn't work." While the water blasting away in the next stall sounded like a torrential downpour, the only hint of water in my stall sounded like a leaky kitchen faucet.

I was determined to wash my car in spite of the obviously malfunctioning hose. For several minutes I soaped down the car with the hose which worked like one of those tiny dental waterpicks. Washing the car inch by inch was tedious work.

I switched the machine dial to RINSE and the feeble trickle continued. I was relentless in my quest to have a clean car. By the time the woman next to me was backing her spotlessly clean car out of the car wash, my car was smeared with an unattractive combination of mud, soap streaks and waterspots.

When I turned to watch the departing car, my hand accidentally slipped downward on the wand. Caught off guard, I realized my mistake as I was thrown backward and nearly off my feet. I had never considered looking for a trigger which would send water spewing all over the place. One split microsecond later, the water stopped. I had used up all of my alloted time.

There was nothing else to do but drive my car out of the car wash as discreetly as possible and hope that no one had witnessed my comedy of errors. I had learned a valuable lesson, however. The next time my car needs to be washed, I'll have someone else do it.

Clothes Encounters

No one can accuse me of being a clothes horse. My wardrobe, which dates back to 1957, could best be described as early rummage sale.

Because my weight tends to fluctuate like a yo-yo, my closet contains clothing which spans at least four sizes. I have perhaps the only wardrobe around which includes Nehru collars and crinolines from the fifties. If time travel should ever become a reality, I would be well prepared.

All of my clothing purchases must meet two requirements: they must be on sale at half-price and they should need little or no ironing. The fact that a sweater may be orange and the skirt magenta seems to have little bearing on my clothing selections.

This week I came across a newspaper article entitled "A Peek into the Closets of the Pros." One woman in the article said of her wardrobe, "I try to buy four to five new outfits each season, and that covers me from Monday to Friday."

If having an outfit means that everything goes together, I don't have one. Whenever I dress for some special occasion, I don't rely on some special bought-to-match outfit. Instead, I throw on this and that and pray that the lighting in the restaurant will be dim.

The woman in the article talked about her Ralph Lauren sweaters and her Gloria Vanderbilt ensembles as though they were personal acquaintances. I've noticed lately that more people are referring to articles of clothing by their brand names, as in "Has anyone seen my Calvin Kleins?" instead of "Has anyone seen my jeans?"

In my spartan wardrobe, jeans are jeans. Somehow it doesn't have the same ring when I ask, "Has anyone seen my discount store jeans?" Rather than being status symbols, my clothing labels merely scratch the back of my neck or cause incessant itching at my waistline. There is little or no status in having a perpetual itch.

With the expenses of having two daughters in college, I am temporarily left with limited choices in clothing. Given the alternatives of being well dressed or well fed, I will opt for the latter. What good is an outfit if I am too weak from hunger to wear it? Sitting down to a platter of roast beef seems vastly more important than looking like a fashion model.

I imagine that I will spend the rest of my life looking like my clothes have been thrown together like so many ingredients in a tossed salad. As long as my clothes are clean and the buttons and seams are intact, I can see little reason to complicate my wardrobe any further by making more purchases.

I can only hope that Nehru collars and starched crinolines will someday make a comeback.

Drive-up Deliveries

Our 21-year-old daughter had surgery this past week. It wasn't as serious as a brain surgery or a total organ transplant, but I must admit that I got a bit excited about the whole ordeal.

After I heard about the plans for surgery, I took pen in hand and jotted down the nice things I would do for her during her hospital stay. I would send her flowers. I would find her a nice gown. I would finally be able to throw out all of those things she has been accumulating under her bed for two decades.

As it turned out, she had one of those same day surgeries. Same day surgeries mean that instead of having surgery and moaning and groaning for nurses for a few days, you have surgery and go home to do your moaning and groaning.

My only stays in hospitals were the times that I had babies. My mother thought it was fairly radical for me to come home after five days. When she had me, she lay on a bed for two weeks and wasn't allowed to walk. By the time she had regained the strength in her legs after that long confinement, I was about three years old. My mother spent about half of her married life recuperating from the births of her five children.

My stays in hospitals were just the right length of time. I languished about and my main concerns with life were manicures, pedicures and soap opera plots on the television. The perks of staying in a hospital were the main reasons I chose to have so many children. Changing diapers and walking the floor at nights were small prices to pay for delicious meals, backrubs and hours of leisure time.

As proof of this point, I've noticed that families are becoming smaller now that postnatal stays are shorter. Without the fringe benefits of a hospital stay, women are calling it quits after only one or two children.

If the current trend continues, it might become possible for maternity patients in the future to use drive-up services at hospitals, not unlike the fast food restaurants of today. Working mothers might be able to have their babies during their lunch hours and not be docked in pay.

I have seen mothers lately as they leave the hospital within a day of giving birth. The back seats of their cars are filled with the bobbing heads of their other children plus assorted other relatives. For all I know, they head straight for the kitchen when they get home and make a seven-course dinner for a crowd of 30. By nightfall, they have probably stripped all of the kitchen floor wax and have canned 12 dozen quarts of peaches.

One-day hospital stays don't necessarily mean progress. Patients shouldn't be required to leave their hospital beds until they have stayed at least five days or at least had that many backrubs. That's why they're called patients, not impatients. What's the rush?

Cotton Makes a Comeback

In terms of cotton clothing, my life has come full-circle. The era of wash-and-wear was dawning in the 1960's when I opted for a life of married bliss. Soon after we had exchanged our vows, I discovered that my husband's wardrobe consisted mostly of 20 long-sleeved, white cotton shirts. During our honeymoon and the second week of non-stop ironing, I realized that the wonderful world of wash-and-wear would not be mine until his troublesome shirts were (a) stolen (b) lost or (c) destroyed. I chose the latter plan of action.

I've never enjoyed ironing. On my priority list, it ranks right down there with cleaning the bathroom bowl and changing the paper  in a bird cage. I approached the mass destruction of his wrinkled shirts with an ingenious plan. My strategy would be amazingly simple. His shirts would appear to die a natural death and they would be replaced with that wonder of the decade, wash-and-wear shirts.

While my husband was out of the house one day, I soaked all 20 of the shirts in a practically 100-percent bleach solution. After they were dried (for the last time!) on the clothesline, they were given a final ironing and put back into the closet.

During the next few weeks, my husband became

very unsettled about his streak of misfortunes with the white shirts. Long, jagged tears appeared without warning down the backs of his shirts, and buttons were falling off with a regular consistency. He was developing a distrust of his favorite old shirts, which were actually falling off his back.

After his second button had fallen off in one day, I innocently suggested that he might like to take advantage of the sale downtown on wash-and-wear shirts. With those new purchases, new horizons were opened to us. The dreaded iron was relegated to the back of the kitchen closet with the pants stretchers and the spray starch. We were dressing completely in plastic clothing before long. Of course there were the constant dangers of melt-down and static electricity, but I was proud to be a member of a non-ironing society.

When our children were little, we dressed them in adorable polyester outfits. With the exception of the people in it, our house was furnished completely in synthetics. We had plastic countertops, plastic furniture (which looked like real wood), plastic draperies and plastic dishes. Actually now that I think about it, our home looked like an oversized Barbie Dream House.

If you will pardon the expression, cotton began cropping up in our lives during this past year. Our daughters have become converts to cotton, and based on their conversations, one would gather that they are the official spokesmen for the cotton industry. They like to look wrinkled and disheveled. Those are words of terror to someone who participated in the annihilation of cotton shirts some 24 years ago in hopes of a better life for all of us.

Ironically, they seen to enjoy ironing their shirts, skirts and dresses. As I watch them bent over the ironing board, faced with towering piles of wrinkled clothing, I can only shake my head in awe and disbelief.

Wedding Dresses

It is almost a certainty that our daughters will marry someday. Marriage has proven to be so popular that some people have tied the knot as many as two or three times.

When each of our three daughters was born, our friends would joke, "Better start saving for another wedding!"

We laughed with them. How absurd! How expensive could a wedding be? We continued to laugh as the girls grew older. Raising children requires a good sense of humor.

Our carefree attitude toward wedding costs was diminished this week when we read a newspaper blurb about the cost of Japanese wedding gowns. According to the article, Japanese brides spend $3,000 to $4,000 on their wedding garments. The article further stated that this figure is four times as great as the amount spent by U.S. and European brides.

A person doesn't have to be a mathematical wizard to figure out that this sets the cost of an American wedding gown somewhere in the neighborhood of $800 to $1,000.

I believe that we have been fairly good sports about our daughters' clothing. When they insisted that life would not be quite the same without designer jeans, designer sweaters and designer socks, we tried to be understanding.

After all, we reasoned, those clothes could be worn indefinitely and we could justify spending a little bit more.

A wedding gown is a different story. It is worn for a couple of hours and then is relegated to a shelf in the closet. It's impractical to plan on wearing it more than once. A wedding gown can't be worn to the grocery store or to Tupperware parties, unless the woman has a penchant for being overdressed.

I rented my wedding dress. An enterprising woman in my hometown bought used wedding dresses and bridesmaid dresses by the armloads. As she added wedding gowns to her swelling collection, she became recognized as a scavenger of nylon taffeta and fluffy netting. For a mere $45, I was able to rent a wedding gown and four bridesmaid dresses.

The dress served its purpose for a couple of hours, and I suppose that dozens of other blushing brides also managed to find happiness with the same dress.

I can't imagine buying a wedding dress with the same amount of money that could buy a quarter of beef or a good, used car. Unless someone in our area sets up a wedding dress rental business in the next few years, we might be forced to explore other alternatives.

I could get out the old sewing machine and practice sewing. As I recall, my home economics teacher once gave me a mediocre grade for my creative efforts with a hemmed dish towel, so that course of action might prove to be less than satisfactory.

Through the use of trick photography, our daughters could be encouraged to stand behind some cardboard cutouts of wedding dresses, creating the illusion of being properly attired. It could be a novel breakthrough in wedding traditions.

Another unlikely possibility would be to have the three girls share the same wedding dress. Since they can't agree on music or movies, there is a very slim chance that they would agree on one dress.

Perhaps our friends were right, after all. We might have to start saving.

My Son, the Dustball

There is one more reason not to dust. Surprisingly enough, this discovery was made last week while I toured the Museum of Anthropology in Mexico City with 15 of my Spanish students.

We were introduced to the gigantic stone sculpture of Coatlicue, the Aztec earth goddess. On a beauty scale of one to ten, she would have scored dismally, especially since her head consisted of two intertwining serpents.

According to Aztec legend, Coatlicue was a remarkable mother and a fastidious housekeeper. After giving birth to the moon and the stars, no simple feats, she busied herself chasing after dustballs in her heavenly domain. The moon's birth announcement would have read: "Coatlicue proudly announces the arrival of a son, the moon. Birth weight: 81 quintillion tons."

On one occasion, Coatlicue collected dustballs, placed them in her apron and headed for the door. However, before she had a chance to throw the dustballs outside, they clumped together and became her new son, the warrior god Huitzilopochtli.

As I stared in awe at the mammouth statue of the snake-headed woman clutching the little warrior god to her chest, many questions about their relationship were left unanswered by our tour guide.

For example, if Coatlicue had chosen to name her dustball offspring Joe or Harold, would he still have become a warrior god? I would imagine that having a name like Huitzilopochtli would give a kid a good reason to be a troublemaker. It would be similar to being a boy named Sue.

Huitzilopochtli also became a manifestation of the sun, and as such his battle against the forces of night was neverending. In other words, he was constantly fighting with his siblings, the moon and the stars. Each morning the sun was born anew, according to the Aztecs, and each night, his combat with the moon and the stars was re-enacted.

In addition to having to worry about dusting and other household chores, Coatlicue had to endure endless fighting among her children. Life must have seemed unbearable at times, as she cleaned up the house every morning after intergalactic spats.

Aztec legends don't mention whether or not Huitzilopochtli was ever sent to school, but Coatlicue would have dreaded parent-teacher conferences. A warrior god would tend to be a disruptive student in any classroom.

Rather than run the risk of having a warrior god constantly underfoot, I will continue my own personal war against dusting or vacuuming. I would much rather have dustballs under the living room sofa than have a child facing possibly 12 or more years of detention and in-school suspension.

Thank you, Coatlicue, for an important, time-saving lesson.

Daytime Soaps

Now that "Search for Tomorrow" has been taken off daytime television, I might be able to talk with my mother. For 35 years the popular soap-opera served as my rival for my mother's attention.

While I was in grade school, and later in high school, "Search for Tomorrow" was unfortunately aired during my school noon hours.

"Shhh!" my mother would admonish me as I ran into the house. "The soup's on the stove. Joanne has just had a miscarriage." Meaningful mother-daughter conversations were impossible as long as the Tate family ruled the air waves.

All of my lunch hours were variations on the same theme. It might have been bologna sandwiches along with the anguish of Arthur Tate's amnesia, or it would be leftover spaghetti and Patty Tate's scandalous affair with her college professor.

As I returned to school after each noon hour, my last impression of my mother would be the back of a woman in a house dress, hunched up close to a black-and-white television set, with her eyes riveted to the fuzzy screen.

Our nighttime meals would serve as instant replays of the lives of the Tate family. My father's job and any details from our real lives would take second place to the Tate family's brushes with scandal, death, love and rare diseases.

For a long time, I was convinced that the Tates and their neighbors, Stu and Marge, were relatives because

Mother talked about them so often.

Our own lives could have been collapsing about our shoulders, but for one-half hour a day, Mother was out of touch with reality. Occasionally, I would test her level of consciousness.

"I failed my history test today, Mom."

"That's nice, dear. Isn't Stu Berman a wonderful man?"

She really wasn't a bad mother. Our cookie jar was always filled, our clothes were always clean and our house was immaculate by most people's standards. My crinoline skirts were always starched.

However, for 30 minutes every weekday, Mother's world consisted solely of Joanne's domestic problems and Ajax Cleanser commercials.

Mother's moods fluctuated madly with the soap-opera scripts. If the show featured a wedding, Mother would be blissfully happy. If a principal character would die or be missing in a plane crash, she would be depressed for the rest of the day.

If our school would have scheduled different noon hours, I believe that my mother and I might have become closer over the years. I am equally convinced that when the last show aired, Mother wore black.

Newspaper Models

News item: "Attention journalists and stockbrokers: Jockey International Inc. is eager to find "real people" in the news business and stock market to model underwear and sprotswear in ads."

Although I have only worked with weekly newspapers, I have yet to meet a newspaper person whom I would like to see scantily dressed in an underwear ad. The mere idea of opening up a newpaper at the dinner table and seeing a news person from my past or present staring out at me in cute little briefs is not a pretty picture.

In all fairness, I must state that being in the newspaper business could be hazardous to anyone's appearance. Take waistlines, for example. There are appearances at banquets given by cattlemen, dairymen and pork producers. There are annual dinners given by the Chamber of Commerce, the Rotary Club and other civic groups. When I left my job as newspaper editor five years ago, and traded the banquet circuit for the classroom, my body went through a mashed potato withdrawal.

Another dangerous aspect of working in a newpaper office consists of office birthdays. I have yet to see a newspaper office where staff birthdays are not celebrated with decorated cakes. I have eaten so many cakes in the back rooms of newspaper offices that I'm convinced that some people have three or four birthdays a year. At other times I have seen newspaper offices supplied with more sweet rolls and doughnuts then the local bakeries.

When I left the newspaper office, I looked less like Lois Lane and more like a beached whale.

I also believe that a model for underwear and sportswear should have a nice tan. It's pretty hard to look like a bronzed god or goddess when you spend most of the daylight hours under fluorescent lights. Given those circumstances, there would be little distinction between where the white underwear stops and the pasty white body takes over.

A model should also look young and refreshed. Writing obituaries, traffic reports, editorials and cooking columns week after week and describing sewer project updates would take their toll on any person's appearance.

Someone should warn Jockey before it's too late and their stock begins to plummet. The idea could give new meaning to the term "news briefs".

A friend once told me that there are two things which should never be seen: sausage being made and the legislature while it's in session. One more category should now be added to his list. Judging from my build and those of my colleagues, you should never see "real people" from the newspaper business in their underwear.

The Fourth Estate might well become the banned estate.

The Dorm Bill

Our second daughter has received a bill for dormitory damages for the past year. The college bill came as a great surprise because she is probably one of the neatest people I've known. At home, her bedroom has been impeccable and she's the kind of person who squeezes from the bottom of the toothpaste tube.

The bill was carefully itemized. It included charges for missing wastebaskets and electrical cords. Extra cleaning charges were included for messes in the dormitory involving squashed pumpkins, yogurt, margarine and catsup. Some other messes were graphically described but are not suitable material for younger audiences. The bill also listed two broken chairs.

I tried to remain calm and collected when I called our daughter that evening.

"So, what's all this business about yogurt and margarine messes at college?" I barked into the phone. I was finding it difficult to adjust to the fact that our daughter had adopted the lifestyle of a common vandal.

After we talked for a while, she reassured me that every resident in the dormitory was being assessed charges for the messes created by a couple of students. It was true. Her pro-rated share of the damages had only amounted to $3.77. Her share of the yogurt mess had been seven cents.

"It was the kids on the fourth floor," she added. It was easier to believe that a faceless group of rowdy students had caused the problem, rather than that my daughter had picked up the habit of fingerpainting on the hall walls with catsup, yogurt and margarine. For all I know, the fourth floor students are explaining to their confused parents that it was all the fault of students on the other floors.

Before the school year began, we had paid a housing deposit of $25 in case such incidents would occur. A note accompanying the damage bill was equally disturbing.

"The amount that you owe at this time to balance your account is $3.77," read the note. "If your account is not balanced by August 21, your housing arrangements for the coming year may be jeopardized."

It was obviously not just an idle threat. If our daughter doesn't send in her payment, she may be throwing away her college education. Without a degree or a place to live, she may be destined to live on street grates in some large city. It's not a pretty picture, but no one said college would be easy.

Credit Cards

Now that our daughters are in college and are as financially insecure as they will be during their entire lives, they have begun to hear from credit card companies.

So far this summer, they have received enough credit card application forms in the mail to wallpaper a small room. If they were to receive all of the cards promised them, they would have to carry small suitcases instead of purses, and they would rattle when they walk. They would have so much plastic on them that they would become chronic victims of static cling. On extremely hot days, they would be in danger of a possible meltdown.

Our oldest daughter has already accumulated cards from every retail and catalog business west of the Mississippi River. She has so many cards that if she were to spend the credit limit on each one, she would have spent close to the amount of our national deficit.

She assures us that it's all right to carry credit cards, as long as you don't use them. She operated under the theory that credit cards should only be used in cases of emergency.

It's a frightening thought, because we're not sure what constitutes an emergency. If the weather turns chilly, will she need a mink coat? If the car gets a flat tire, will she need a new Porsche?

We're talking about the same daughter who only a few, short years ago discovered that when I wrote checks at the grocery store, I was spending real money. Until then, she thought I received groceries in exchange for my autograph.

The credit card companies really aren't at fault. Before these college students go into lucrative fields like teaching, the companies feel obligated to tell them about the good life.

They want all of us to live in tastefully appointed homes, to drive in classy cars and to dress in fashions direct from the Paris showrooms. They want only the best for us. It's certainly not their fault if we have to sell our bodies for medical research, subsist on boullion cubes or sell the family Bible in order to pay the monthly bills.

The companies have changeable moods. While one month they may be pleading for you to use their cards ("We've missed your business...may we help you?"), the next month they may be issuing veiled threats about sending you to Death Row. Their application letters may sound like love letters, but their follow-up bills resemble traffic court summonses.

Long before Faun Hall made shredding a popular household word, I cut up most of our credit cards into sharp, plastic slivers. It was a fairly painful ordeal, but we survived. We became accustomed to carrying checks and cash.

I didn't realize how much credit cards had taken over our lives until I checked into a motel in the Twin Cities last summer. As I paid for my room with crisp, twenty-dollar bills, the desk clerk eyed me suspiciously and asked, "Do you have any identification?"

The Garbage Can

A garbage can has come between my daughters and me. It wasn't a difference over curfews, phone privileges or the use of the car which divided us, but rather a 20-gallon galvanized steel garbage can.

It was a necessary purchase. We have discovered through cruel experience that plastic trash bags left outside are fair play for the roving dogs of the neighborhood. As they meandor through the dark on their appointed rounds, they have unfortunately discovered that our trash bags can be as much fun as a day at Valleyfair.

Two of our teenaged daughters accompanied me to one of those discount stores which sell everything under the sun. It wasn't my fault that we grabbed a shopping cart with squeaking wheels at the entrance to the store. Neither was it my fault that the garbage cans were displayed at the far back end of the five-acre store.

The girls have always been good sports when it comes to shopping for harmless articles like groceries, shampoo and clothing. However, they couldn't seem to come to grips with the purchase of a garbage pail. Our youngest daughter was the first to realize that there might be some logistics problem as I tried to pile that 20-gallon pail atop the five-gallon shopping cart.

"You're going to have to carry that thing to the front of the store." Granted, and it was my intent that she would help me with the shopping cart. The older of the two girls had already appraised the situation and had long vanished from sight. She was presumably brows-

139

ing around the cosmetics department, ready to disavow any knowledge of me in case anyone should ask.

"Mom, I know people in this store!" pleaded the younger daughter. But I was not a woman to be bargained with, for I could envision the neighbor's dogs frolicking through our table scraps and potato peelings.

She soon disappeared behind some aisle displays and I was abandoned with the shopping cart and the garbage pail. At that moment, I strongly empathized with Benedict Arnold's mother.

It took me about twenty minutes to finally make it to the check-out counter. Taking my time, I stopped periodically to check out certain specials in the store. Each of my stops was accompanied by the clanking of the garbage pail and the screech-screech of the shopping cart wheels. I stopped at the displays of sale clothing (clank-clank, screech-screech), toothpaste (clank-clank), and bargain cassette tapes (clank-clank, screech-screech).

In spite of the bulky garbage can, which seemed to bump into every display and encouraged stares from the other shoppers, I had a lovely time. My daughters had apparently vanished from the face of the earth.

As I finally stood quietly in the check-out line, they magically rematerialized behind me. Their ability to disappear and reappear from sight will continue to mystify me.

As I prepared to fling the garbage can onto the counter, the line was closed by a check-out girl eager to have her coffee break. For one more awkward moment, I was required to move my purchases (clank-clank, screech-screech) to another lane. Then I had to hoist the can above my head to get it through the narrow check-out aisle.

It was one of those "Mother, I-could-just-die" situations.

The Chauffeur

For the first time in 21 years, my husband and I are no longer chauffeurs. When our youngest daughter received her driving license this past week, I was sure that I could hear the Hallelujah chorus from Handel's *Messiah*. Church bells rang and there were fireworks.

Decades ago, when we first decided to become parents, we had no idea that the job description of a parent included logging enough miles to circle the earth several times.

We started innocently with memorable treks to nursery school, the doctor and the dentist. We soon found ourselves driving to Scout meetings, Little League games and dancing lessons. The business of being a chauffeur seemed to snowball, and we were making trips on a routine basis to the orthodontist, play rehearsals, school concerts, ball games, the movies and the swimming pool.

During the last few years, we have learned more about the front entry to the local high school than we cared to know. While we waited for our passengers after school, we were able to memorize every crack in the sidewalk, every shrub and every other parent's car. Through rain, sleet, snow and sweltering heat, we have driven enough miles to make a long-distance trucker turn green with envy.

We have gone through countless station wagons and cars with four doors in the pursuit of transporting our daughters from one place to another. We needed larger cars to lug around the band instruments, sleeping bags, school books and other necessary equipment.

In our hearts we have always thought of ourselves as two-bucket-seat people. Deep down inside, we knew that we were meant to drive sporty low-slung, little cars with four-on-the-floor and very little practicality. Except for our responsibilities as chauffeurs, I could have been Isadora Duncan in her wire-wheeled sports car and my husband could have been Mario Andretti.

For the sake of being parents, we gave up life in the fast lane for backseats full of groceries and the familiar command, "Get in the car, kids, we're going to town!"

The life we chose may not have been as exciting as the Indianapolis 500 or as a scene from *The Great Gatsby*, but it was nevertheless rewarding. We will undoubtedly miss the bickering between sisters as they were carted from one destination to another and the heated debates about who would sit next to the window.

They were the best of times and they were the worst of times. My only fear is that by the time we manage to buy a sportier car, we will no longer be able to bend down to get into the seats.

The Nerd

I can't recall the exact moment I began dressing like a nerd. While I was in high school back in the fifties, nerds, as we called them, were easily identified. Their clothes were mismatched prints and colors, wrinkled fabrics, high-top tennis shoes and high water pants.

Although my friends and I dismissed them as people marching to different drummers, it now appears that they were anticipating fashions thirty years beyond their time. Surprisingly, many of the nerds went on to become religious leaders, doctors and scientists, but that's a different story.

The point I wanted to make is that we were extremely clothes-conscious. Our clothes were carefully pressed and my friends and I read *Seventeen* religiously. Given a choice, we would prefer to stand and not risk having wrinkles in our clothing. We dusted our white buck shoes with chalkboard erasers between classes in order to cover up unsightly scuff marks. In an era before plastic clothing and wash-and-wear fabrics, we were committed to looking impeccably neat.

A young man came to our door this summer, asking for one of our daughters. He appeared to be the reincarnation of a 1950's nerd. He wore a terminally wrinkled Hawaiian print shirt with striped shorts. Tired looking socks drooped over the tops of his grungy, high-top tennis shoes, which obviously had been white at one time in the distant past.

After taking a quick glance at his attire, I pulled my daughter aside and spoke with her in hushed tones.

"Don't look now, but...DON'T LOOK NOW!..but his boxer shorts are showing at least two inches beneath the bottom of his shorts! Who is this person anyway?"

"But, Mom", my daughter explained, "that's 'in'".

"It's 'in' to have your underwear showing in public?

143

And look at his clothes! They're so wrinkled it looks like he sleeps in them!"

"But, Mom, they're designer clothes. He's supposed to look that way."

"So who's his designer? Boxcar Willie? He looks like a nerd to me." My ranting continued. "If this is well dressed, what do the nerds look like?"

"Oh, they wear polyester and they look really boring." She pronounced "boring" as if it had three syllables. "Bo-or-ing".

"Oh", I murmured. I glanced down at my own clothes which were carefully color-coordinated and contained at least ninety-nine percent polyester and other synthetics.

"Like this?" I asked as I pointed at my own outfit.

"Yes, that's what the nerds wear." She paused a beat and then added diplomatically, "But it's okay for mothers to dress like that, though". I suddenly felt much older.

Raking Leaves

Raking the leaves is one of those endless jobs, like putting a child through college or playing a complicated game like Monopoly with a three-year-old.

It also puts a person under considerable pressure. In our city, for example, a few weeks are set aside each fall for the pickup of leaves. Whether or not those designated dates coincide with the time the leaves fall to the ground is completely up to the whims of Mother Nature and the city fathers.

I missed the first week of leaf pickups because there were no leaves on our yard. Our trees were clinging to their leaves like dates unwilling to part at the end of a perfect evening. Short of climbing the trees and shaking their branches, there was nothing else to do.

At the beginning of the second week, our trees completely shed their leaves. There was no fanfare. They just stood there on a perfectly calm afternoon and dumped about 4,000 cubic tons of leaves on our yard.

I had a fairly positive outlook during the first week of raking. It seemed exhilarating to breathe the crisp autumn air and exercise muscles which hadn't been used since the previous fall. It felt good to be alive and I was reduced to the mindset of a maudlin greeting card.

Perhaps the most satisfying thing of all was gazing out over our yard when the raking was completed and knowing that it had been a job well done. When Michelangelo put away his paint brushes after painting the Sistine Chapel, he couldn't have felt more fulfilled than I did when I put away the rake for another season.

Last week was another matter. The wind came up and our neighbors' magnificent maples dumped on our yard. With the pressure of the last city pickup breathing down my neck, and with a pending sense of doom, I begrudgingly got out the rake again. The prospect of raking leaves had lost its original thrill.

If Socialism means that all members of a society or the community share in the work, raking leaves is a socialist act. I had already raked my leaves; now I was raking theirs. While they no doubt were enthralled when their trees burst into a riot of color in the fall, I had to rake up the aftereffects. It was like not being invited to a party, but having to clean up the mess afterwards.

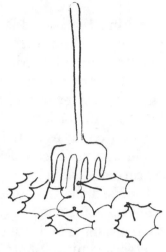

It would have been one thing, I fumed as I raked, if we had been able to see the leaves from our windows during the rest of the year. Let's face it. Those leaves were complete strangers.

I'm not going to rake again this year. Outside of the fact that they will never be picked up, there's a lot to be said for lawn mulching. Perhaps leaves on the lawn aren't all that bad.

It will be a long time before I will be willing to turn over a new leaf.

The Toad

A toad has taken over our basement. Sometime during the summer, when a basement window was open, the prehistoric looking creature literally leaped into our lives.

Our trips into the basement are no longer routine excursions, taken for granted. Simply washing the clothes has become an immense challenge, as we try to carry the clothes baskets while leaping out of the toad's way.

The toad is clever. Whenever my daughter or I go into the basement, the toad can be seen sitting in the middle of the floor, as if it is defying us.

"Go ahead, lady. Make my day. See if you can wash those clothes without stepping on me." Although no words are actually spoken, the toad does a very credible impression of Clint Eastwood. Whenever my husband, who is the chief spider killer and toad exterminator in our house, looks for the toad, it is nowhere to be seen.

As far as my husband knows, the toad is a figment of our imaginations. How can he pursue an invisible quarry? I have described the toad's dimensions, which seem to grow with each telling. My most current report has the toad measuring a foot around and weighing about four pounds.

In order to better understand the uninvited amphibian in our basement, I have researched the toad in our encyclopedia. I hoped that the toad would soon finish its normal lifespan in our basement, since a dead toad would be easier to cope with than a live one. I was disheartened to read that toads can live for as long as 36 years. If that is the case, there is a good possibility that the lumpy-looking creature in our basement will outlive me. If we should ever move, our house will have to be sold with furnace, water softener and a basement protected by an attack toad.

I was further dismayed to read that a toad can change its size whenever it wants to. I can imagine sorting out the laundry someday, and finding a creature the size of Godzilla breathing over my shoulder. The encyclopedia fails to mention how big they can get when they really want to increase their size. I wonder if it would be possible to mistake the toad for the furnace if it should ever get one of its inflationary moods.

Although weeks have gone by, we continue to run the obstacle course from the basement door to the washing machine. We talk loudly to ourselves as we cross the basement floor, in an attempt to scare off the toad. The worst scenario would have one of us stepping on the toad in our bare feet and with an armload of laundry. The chief exterminator in our house is of no help as he greets our laments with a questionable sense of humor.

Last night I had another encounter with the warty creature in our basement. When I complained to my husband, he casually responded, "Haven't you toad me all this before?" When it comes to toads, chivalry is dead.

Storm Windows

If, on the heels of Halloween, someone were to compile a list of the most frightening places to stay, our home would have to be included.

Unlike the Bates Motel in "Psycho", it doesn't have a shower which would send millions of Americans back to the relative security of their bathtubs.

It doesn't have a backyard swimming pool built over a forgotten cemetery like the home did in the movie, "Poltergeist".

Our home doesn't have ghosts, gremlins or spectral images, but it does have something almost as terrifying.

It has storm windows.

After living in houses with combination windows for over 25 years, we now live in a house with storm windows that seem to constantly demand our attention. It would appear that it's part of a perverse scheme to make sure the occupants of the house wash windows at least twice a year.

Actually, it only takes one day to remove the screens and put up the storm windows, and another day to reverse the process. The rest of the year is spent complaining about having to do it or about having just done it.

Our house was built by a misguided contractor, who apparently never washed a window in his life. He mistakenly believed that some people like nothing better than dangling precariously from the top of a stepladder with a storm window under one arm and a bottle of window cleaner and a cleaning rag under the other.

Carrying a storm window around a backyard on a

windy day is much like hang gliding. With the wind at just the right speed and the window held at just the right angle, it would be possible for an unsuspecting mother to be carried aloft for miles and not be missed until the next meal.

When we had those marvelous combination windows, I could do more domestic things for my family. I would use the extra time to prepare frozen pizzas and other gourmet delights.

Because of the cumbersome storm windows, our meals have become virtually non-existent on at least two days of the year. It's bad enough that my family has to miss well-balanced meals on days I wash clothes and on days beginning with S, M, T, W or F.

Storm windows can be real panes.

Cow Boots

Cows are now horning their way into the world of high fashion. It was one thing to learn that farmers in Pennsylvania were feeding their dairy cows broken chocolate candy bars. At that time, I contended that the discarded chocolate could better be shipped to my fellow chocolate lovers.

An English dairy farmer recently outfitted his herd of 125 dairy cows with specially made Wellington boots, at a cost of $24 per boot. He noted that the high-protein diet required by modern dairy-farming stimulates extra growth in the hooves, making them susceptible to cracking during the cows' winter confinement in concrete-floored farmyards. His neighbors are also ordering the boots for their cows.

I now understand the derivation of the term "bossy". Not only are the cows of the world determined to eat our chocolate, they are also hoping to outdo the rest of us in winter apparel. At the rate of their current demands, it wouldn't surprise me to hear that cows are wearing designer jeans and having their forelocks set in the latest styles with crimping irons.

Most of us can only dream of wearing Wellington boots. All a cow has to do, it seems, is to show some sympathetic farmer her split hooves and perhaps blink her big, brown eyes, and she is given not only one pair, but two, of the trendy footwear. I suppose she can't be faulted for having four feet, but it really doesn't seem fair.

I buy most of my winter boots in discount store close-out bins during the late spring. If I'm lucky, I'll be able to find two boots in the same size. My relationships with bargain boots are short-lived affairs, primarily because they fall apart when exposed to rain, snow or cold temperatures. They appear to be designed for looks rather than durability, and they don't look all that great, either.

Why should cows be treated better than people? We eat too much protein, spend our working hours standing on concrete floors and we are also subjected to miserable winter weather. There must be millions of people with split toe nails. So, I ask, where are our Wellington boots? It appears that cows have cornered the market when it comes to sympathy.

First, it was our chocolate, and now it's bovine booties. As long as dairy farmers tend to interpret their "moos" as "mores", cows will continue to live better than the rest of us.

It's only a matter of time before the cows, wearing designer labels and eating our chocolate, will demand VCR's for their milking parlors. Once the screens are in place, they will soon be watching such bovine classics as "Beverly Hills Cow", "West Hide Story", "Back to the Pasture" and "The Sound of Moo-sic."

Some people believe that we return someday in the form of an animal. Although I could never be that lucky, I would like to return as a cow.

Water Rationing

I have always been intrigued by creative threats. My own knack for dispensing swift and sure justice quite naturally led to my decisouns to become a mother and a teacher.

As a mother, I have been able to blurt out profound prophecies, including "If you don't clean your room, you will be grounded for the rest of your natural life" and "Limit those phone calls or I'll rip the cord out of the wall."

Teachers can get by with saying things like "Read Julius Caesar or you will spend the rest of your life in 10th grade." Fortunately, no one to date has bothered to test my threats. No matter how creative I have tried to be, none of my threats could hold a candle to the threats made by many municipalities during this year's drought.

My hometown has instituted an odd-even number system of outdoor water usage. It's a fairly complicated system which involves certain hours of the day and whether you live in a house with an even or uneven number. Although I can't be sure, Zodiacal signs are also figured into the formula. For example of how the system works, if your house number is 315, like ours, you may water you lawn and garden on days with odd numbers during hours that you normally sleep.

The most interesting aspect of the system is the penalty imposed by the powers that be. Following a first warning, any attempts to water a wilting rose bush or some other illegal use of water would result in having one's water turned off completely.

Penalties seem to vary from town to town. A nearby city imposes $100 fines for failure to comply with the rules. If the water shortage should continue, one can only speculate about further measures which will be implemented.

Perhaps a new element in law enforcement will be introduced into our communitites, and instead of having SWAT teams, towns will have 'SWET teams which roam the streets in dark colored vans. Equipped with such high tech equipment as hose cuters and sprinkler crushers, teams will look for suspicious signs of misconduct, including wet sidewalks, shiny cars and unusually green lawns. Gardens yielding tomatoes over one inch in diameter will also be carefully monitored by the 'SWET teams.

Try to imagine the horror of having a 'SWET van pull up in your driveway with its lights flashing and its sirens blaring. As the neighbors would crowd around your house to get a better look, a crack-shot team would reduce your garden hoses to shreds in a matter of seconds and the handles would be blow-torched from all of your outside faucets. Your reputation would be ruined forever and you would become a persona non grata at most Tupperware parties and other important social functions.

If the water shortage should become more intense, it's possible that normally friendly neighbors could becmoe informants. The neighbor who still owes you four cups of sugar and one cup of flour could have your water supply cut off by simply dialing a phone number and making an anonymous tip.

If having a green lawn is a sure sign of guilt, we should be safe from any future arrests. Our lawn is so brown that we have seriously considered spray-painting it green. Our yard has become so parched that I wouldn't be surprised to look out the window and see a caravan of camels pass through someday.

Until I can synchronize my watch and can compute whether the number on our house matches the number of any given day, our lawn is destined to look like the great Sahara.

Designer Sunglasses

When our nephew visited us last summer he did something quite crazy. He bought a pair of sunglasses for $80.

Granted, he's single. He doesn't know about mortgage payments and orthodontist bills. He doesn't worry about the price of ground beef.

My relationships with sunglasses are usually short-lived. Every Memorial Day weekend, I invest in a new, inexpensive pair, and by the end of the first week, I'm left squinting in the sun.

My sunglasses have been sat on, stepped on and left behind in other people's cars. If I do manage to hold on-to a pair for longer than a week, they are usually worthless, anyway. After being carried around in the bottom of my purse with nail files and other lethal objects, the scratched lenses resemble etched glass windows.

Looking at the world through scratched lenses can change your entire perspective. People's faces become lopsided and it's like looking through a child's kaleidoscope. In fact, if I choose to wear them, my vision is so bad that I could be eligible for benefits to the blind.

I was with my nephew when he bought the designer sunglasses. Although, for the money, I would have preferred a quarter of beef or 40 frozen pizzas, he seemed ecstatic with his purchase.

After paying so much for two lenses and a piece of plastic, I would have been too stunned to speak. As he tried them on in the store, with the designer name printed on the lens in front of his left eye, I figured that the company should be paying him to do their advertising.

As we drove home, he raved on about his new sunglasses. It was sort of like buying a new car. Once the decision is made to buy it, you can't say enough good things about it.

He told me how they would protect him from dangerous ultra-violet rays. Judging from the way he talked, the glasses would also ensure world peace and solve the problems of modern society. His new sunglasses were nothing short of a miracle.

Their main virtue seemed to be their special tint, apparently only available in $80 sunglasses and in that particular brand.

"Here! Try them on!" he exclaimed as he drove the car. He seemed overzealous in his attempt to convert me to designer labels.

I tried them on, and in turn, handed him my own El Cheapo sunglasses.

From that point on, we rode in absolute silence. His sunglasses, hand-crafted by French artisans, and mine, mass-produced in Taiwan, had exactly the same tint.

It was a long ride home.

Long Hair

If the fad has already reached St. Louis, we can't be far behind. Are you ready for this? Men are wearing ponytails.

A St. Louis hair stylist describes the new hair style as "short on the top and fuller at the bottom so that he can look good for IBM, yet long enough to pull back into a tail and be ready for a disco."

The *Wall Street Journal* noted, "The lure of the style is partly attitudinal. Men say that the instant they pull their hair back, they feel hip and devilishly liberated."

That's all fine and dandy, but a man shouldn't appear to be too devilish at the grain elevator or when he shows up for coffee at the local bakery.

He might as well wear a dress for the full effect.

The last time anyone hip or devilishly liberated appeared in my hometown, they stopped briefly to fill up their van with gas and then they continued their trip down the interstate.

They had a bumper sticker which read, "Don't laugh-Your daughter may be inside", and they were the main topic of conversation downtown for weeks afterwards.

It's hard to look hip and devilish in a town without a sushi restaurant and the gourmet section in the grocery store carries only bagels and cream cheese.

I doubt whether small towns would adapt well to having their leading male citizens looking like flower children from a bygone era.

Long hair doesn't come without its share of problems. There are enough things to worry about in this world, like jello that doesn't set and ring-around-the-collar. We don't need more hair-clogged drains or the other half of the population complaining about split ends.

We don't have an IBM plant or a disco in our town.

The closest thing we have is a farm store and Saturday night dances at the V.FW.

Any man considering this new fad might very well find himself all tressed up with no place to go.

All About Pi

We will all be able to sleep better at night. Using supercomputers, two Columbia University mathematicians have established a new record for the digits of Pi.

Pi, as you may recall from your school days, is the ratio of the circumference of a circle to its diameter. With dread in my heart, I once referred to it as 3.14.

My geometry teacher allowed us to use the 3.14 in class, but he told us that the numbers actually ran off into infinity. If he is alive today, he is probably very excited that those two mathematicians have printed out the actual Pi up to 280 million digits. Printed out, the numbers would extend for 600 miles.

Although this may be exciting news for a tiny percentage of the world's population, it serves as a personal reminder that I learned absolutely nothing from Pi and the lessons connected with it.

I have been around the block for over four decades, and not one person has stopped me on the street to ask about the ratio of a circumference of a circle to its diameter.

I know that if I would have broached the subject at home, while I was growning up, my mother would have washed out my mouth with soap. To this day, she believes that condominiums shouldn't be discussed in mixed company.

I also gained some other useless knowledge during my student days. Speaking Middle English was a good example. After an entire semester in college, I could spout things like, "We faren as he as dronke as a mous; a dronk man woot well he hath a hoos." Roughly translated, it meant, "We get along like a man who is drunk as a mouse; a drunk man knows well he has a house."

Years rolled by, and I never ran across another human being who had learned those same lines. Finally, at a party, out of the blue, I quoted those words. No one seemed impressed. In fact, the hostess offered me a cup of black coffee and the reassurance that I would soon feel better.

In my seventh grade home economics class, we spent weeks frying sausage patties. My final project, a sausage patty which resembled the head of a mouse with large ears, nearly held me back a year because our teacher was a stickler for symmetrical patties.

I never fried another sausage patty. As a matter of fact, I rarely make breakfasts. Our children were brought up thinking there were only two meals a day.

If they saw a family on television, eating a meal in the morning, I assured them it was only fiction. When they grew older and questioned me further, I explained that we were Protestant. That answer satisfied them until they graduated from high school.

Somewhere, in the cobweb-filled recesses of my brain, are the population figures for the Aleutian Islands and the average annual rainfall for the state of Nevada. Back in there, with other useless facts and information, remains the understanding of Pi.

Holstein Heaven

Bad idea department: Two weeks ago, a luxurious downtown Minneapolis hotel hosted a national Holstein convention. Things turned for the worse when they invited the cows to come inside.

Of the 140 cows and bulls attending the festivities, only a choice few were paraded through the carpeted ballroom for a special auction. As a precautionary measure, the carpet had been covered with wood chips in case any cow would get caught up in the excitement of the moment. The chandeliers were optimistically left uncovered.

I'm surprised that they didn't consider using Kitty Litter. To summarize the situation gently, the bovine conventioneers made a big stink about their accommodations.

After the convention, the cows were led back to greener pastures, but the memory of their visit continues to linger on. Now the hotel is faced with the monumental task of shampooing the carpet and removing the scent of Eau de Cow.

Because I'm reluctant to have even dogs or cats in the house, it seems incredible that the hotel would have decided to entertain a herd of cows. I wonder what kind of madness led to their decision.

Perhaps hotel officials figured that any cow worth $54,000 would undoubtedly be housebroken. Maybe the management expected the bovines and their owners would be udderly fantastic tippers.

Cows are pretty pushy animals. If you doubt that statement, consider for one moment how many cows are named "Bossie." Because of their bullish behavior, it's no wonder that the bovines ignored restroom signs and did whatever they did whenever the spirit moved them.

While we still lived on the farm, we had stock cows

that wanted to come into our house one morning. The sun had barely begun to rise when I awoke to the sound of loud mooing directly outside our first floor bedroom window.

When I rolled over, half asleep, I was greeted by the sight of two black and white cows, their noses pressed to the window glass. Apparently, they had broken through their fence and had decided to conduct a study on the sleeping patterns of humans.

Before matters got out of hand, we chased them back into their proper surroundings. Unlike the Minneapolis hotel, we had no intention of inviting them in for breakfast.

I wonder if the hotel will turn down future applications for conventions from the Holsteins, or if they will allow themselves to be cowed into hosting the event again.

One thing is for sure. If they are allowed to return, the cows shouldn't leave behind their calling cards.

Oatmeal Cologne

Oatmeal cookie will be the new scent in men and women's colognes.

Perfume makers are no longer content with making us smell like musk, lilacs, roses and Jamaican rum. A perfumery in Los Angeles is taking a gamble that we would all like to smell like our mothers kitchens.

If this trend continues, it won't be much longer before we'll be splashing on "eau de spaghetti" and "eau of chili."

The new oatmeal scent might also create its share of domestic unhappiness.

Not long ago, I discovered how disappointing false scents can be. I innocently purchased some room spray that smelled like cinnamon, ginger and other spices normally associated with home baking.

When my husband came home from work that evening, his face lit up and he exclaimed, "Oh! You've baked! Something smells good!"

"It's only a room spray," I apologized.

A pall was immediately cast over our entire evening. There is evidently nothing more disconcerting than being surrounded by the scent of spices and not being able to eat cookies that deliver the same flavor.

The spicy scent no doubt triggered vague memories in my husband's mind of the days, ages ago, when I used to bake. He has a memory like a steel trap.

It's been so long since I've baked, that I'm not even sure where the cookie sheets are.

In fact, if a burglar were to steal off into the night with my stove, I probably wouldn't notice for weeks.

I can't help but think that the spice scented room spray has sent other families scurrying off to empty cookie jars. Room sprays and colognes shouldn't trigger people's appetites and play tricks with their minds.

I wouldn't dream of placing one of those simmering

potpourris on the back burner. The scent would drive my family over the edge.

Actually, in the time that it takes to get out a pan, fill it with water and add the potpourri, you could probably whip up a batch of cookies and have the real thing.

When it comes to wearing a cologne that smells like oatmeal cookies, I'll have to pass.

I would much rather have my husband think about something else besides cookies when I walk into the room.

The Miraculous Power Outage

One day after work this week, I drove home to a house without electricity. At 4:30 in the afternoon, our neighborhood was powerless as the city crews did some work with the electrical lines. While the power outage must have played havoc in many homes, with cooks staring blankly at half-baked potatoes and meat loaves, I considered the occasion to be a miracle.

With the simple flicking of a switch, the city had given us a wonderful excuse to eat out.

Being a double-income family does have its drawbacks. Take, for example, the matter of nighttime meals. Gone forever are the days when I would spend half the afternoon paring potatoes and clipping interesting recipes out of grocery counter magazines.

Because both of us work, and the dinner preparation time has been reduced to a few precious minutes, I no longer worry about attractive table settings and menus which would make the world's chefs green with envy. More likely than not, my biggest decision is whether to bake a frozen pizza or a couple of those prepackaged microwave dinners.

Our last regular weekday dinner took place on October, 1987, which also happened to be a rare, sick day from work. I had fallen down the stairs and sprained my ankle. Out of sheer boredom, I hobbled around the kitchen on crutches and prepared a real meal, which my husband now refers to nostalgically as his Last Supper.

Except for days when I'm home, running a raging fever or overcoming some rare disease, our nighttime meals have become dismal affairs. We have become accustomed to food which tastes like their cardboard containers. I have exhausted the 15-minute meals printed on the boxes of instant rice and there's only so much that one can do with a slow-cooking crock pot.

Although eating out still seems like an extravagance, we did manage to eat out this week. Without electrical power for the oven or the microwave, our possibilities for eating became severely limited. The refrigerator was our only ray of hope for a decent meal, and I had serious doubts about putting a meal together with a jar of diet mayonnaise, half a bottle of catsup and a handful of icecubes.

There were also some small dishes hidden in the back shelves of the refrigerator which had grown layers of green fuzz, but I decided to save those mysteries for some future archeologist who wishes to study the eating habits of 20th century Minnesotans.

So we ate out and I treated. Unlike many double-income couples, we don't squabble about His money and Her money. We don't play games about who's paying for what. Whatever I earn is mine and whatever he earns is mine. Only one person can be unhappy with this arrangement.

When the city turned off our electricity, I began to believe in miracles.

The Dustballs

(News item: "One in five Americans rearrange their furniture monthly, says a survey by Spiegel, Inc.")

If it weren't for dustballs, I would probably rearrange our furniture more often. As you may be aware, dustballs are aggregated clumps of dust, loose hair and lint that settle under furniture, behind doors and in other out-of-the-way breeding areas. 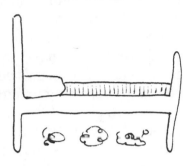 They are the number one household pest, followed closely by box elder bugs.

The dustballs in our house seem to have a life of their own. In fact, a few dustballs now residing under our couch are so large and active they should be wearing flea collars. Sometimes, late at night, when I pretend to be preoccupied with a book, I can see them slithering about the corners of the room, casting furtive looks in my direction.

Vacuuming the floors and rearranging furniture have never been high on my list of priorities. It has always seemed more important to have meals on the table and clean clothes on our backs. Waging an all-out war on dustballs has forever seemed like an exercise in futility.

Getting rid of a dustball is much like pulling out a stray gray hair. You remove it, and a dozen others appear in its place. It's like shoveling the driveway while it's still snowing. Dustballs multiply as a faster rate than the proverbial rabbit.

Once you have grown used to furniture being in a certain arrangement, it's very unsettling to discover that your recliner chair has been replaced by a glass-topped coffee table. That's perhaps the number one reason why I am reluctant to move the furniture around. On one occasion, when I decided to give our bedroom a new look, I moved the bed to the other side of the room. When I woke up the next morning, I walked directly into a wall. Old habits are hard to break.

The second reason why I don't move the furniture is that I would also have to dust and vacuum. When I move a chair that hasn't been moved for months, I run the risk of upsetting an entire colony of dustballs. In a system, which could well be adopted by confronting nations, I don't bother them and they don't bother me.

Once the chair is moved, and I receive the startled stares of the dustballs, I can no longer deny they exist. I can recall my mother's admonishment, "Cleanliness is next to Godliness", and I have no other recourse except to find the vacuum cleaner in its last hiding place and exterminate the little devils. Using the vacuum is no simple matter, either. On the rare occasions that I use it, I have to get out the user's manual to refresh my memory.

In light of bigger problems like the national debt, I try my best to avoid direct confrontations with dustballs. Rather than engaging in outright dustball genocide, I would prefer to follow that old axiom, "Out of sight, out of mind."

Today's Pet is Tomorrow's Pork Chop

I have always had mixed feelings about house pets. Although many of our friends have dogs and cats, which have become members of their families, I have no desire to hear the patter of little paws around our house. Horrifying stories about hairballs in the stomachs of cats, surprise litters of puppies and ongoing battles with cat litter boxes have contributed to our decision to remain petless.

Instead of pets, we had children. Once we had outgrown the problems of overturned glasses of milk at the dinner table and toys strewn about the house, we were no longer in the mood for shedding pet hair and whining demands to be let outside.

It was surprising to read that pet fanciers are no longer content with run-of-the-mill pets like cats, goldfish and dogs. Miniature pigs are now invading American homes as household pets. Arnold the Pig is no longer a joke.

These popular pets, officially known as Chinese potbelly pigs, are fullgrown at 60 pounds, or roughly the size of your average second-grader. Although they had originally been confined to the pig lots of Asian peasants for hundreds of years,  they are now grunting their approval of a new lifestyle in family rooms across the country.

I can't imagine having a pig as a household pet. A person should have a pet that has pleasant associations with its breed. For instance, whenever I see a Saint Bernard, I think of others like it, rescuing stranded skiiers and mountain climbers in the Alps and other remote places. It is inconceivable that a pig could ever take the place of man's best friend.

At best, my associations with pigs include bacon, pork chops and holiday hams. I wouldn't feel right somehow about stroking a pet pig's neck while his distant relative is languishing nearby in a 325-degree oven.

As I see it, one of the advantages of having pets is their ability to consume table leftovers. Feeding leftover breakfast bacon and pork chop bones to a pet pig would be like contributing to the practice of cannibalism.

Being treated like a pet might be wonderful from a pig's perspective, but it could cause irreparable damage to the pork industry. The idea of eating anything that resembles a family pet could be a real turn-off to many people. They would no more eat pork than they would eat kitty burgers or actual hot dogs.

If this pet pig fad continues, we can also expect to see homes with pet chickens and other miniaturized farm animals. With pet pigs greeting us at the door, we would no longer be able to come home from work and proclaim, "There's nothing to eat in the house." Today's pet could become tomorrow's main course.

High Tech Garbage

Our city has a new garbage collection system. Actually, it is now called refuse collection, but garbage is garbage is garbage. Garbage by any other name would still smell the same.

The new garbage recycling plan is complex to say the least. In order to follow the complicated instructions, a person would need a law degree, if not a degree in garbology.

A half-page ad explaining the new system ran in the local newspaper, complete with a map, outlining the new collection routes. One black boundary line ran through what at first appeared to be our living room, and I was in a real quandry.

However, my husband, a former Boy Scout, got out his trusty compass and figured out our pickup date. It helped when he turned the map right side up. Map reading has never been one of my virtues.

Boiled down to its finer points, which roughly resemble the length of a doctoral dissertation, the plan has us doing something with our garbage most days of the week. At our house, for example, lawn clippings and garden wastes go out one day, twigs and garbage on another and all newspapers are to be set out on the curb, in neat bundles, on the first Saturday of each month. As I see it, I will be spending more time sorting out garbage than I spend with my family.

As a direct result of the new sorting system, our back porch now resembles a laboratory for the research of landfill materials. Our piles of garbage show more organization than our closets do.

The new system has a few holes. For example, with our newspapers, twigs and garbage all going off in different directions, what shall we do about hazardous wastes? On the first day of the new system, I noticed that our neighbors had been left with a rejected can of paint on their front curb. This might mean that we will have to transport our paint cans to a hazardous waste site in either Provo, Utah, or Pueblo, Colorado.

There is also a thin line between my cooking attempts and hazardous wastes. If my family refuses to eat some exotic casserole dish, there is also a good chance that the city might red-tag the leftovers. A person can only take so much rejection.

My credo for life, until the new system, had been "If you can't eat it, wear it or pass it off as a white elephant gift, throw it in the garbage." If the trash is good enough to gift wrap, I wouldn't be putting it in the garbage can in the first place.

My biggest problem with the new recycling plan was that it was revealed after I had already accumulated three full bags of nonstandard garbage. For almost a week I had filled the bags with reckless abandon. I had mixed coffee grounds, tin cans, egg shells and newspapers with little thought to environmental issues or the quality of life for future generations. My only recourse would have been to dump it all out on the kitchen floor and sort it. Instead, I chose to run the risk of serving a jail sentence, paying a fine, or both.

Things could be worse. The city could be asking us to rinse off our garbage before it's placed in the bags.

The Appraisal

I had always marveled how some couples, once their children have grown, manage to squeeze all of their belongings from a spacious home into a small apartment. The reason is now crystal clear. Whenever their children come home for a visit, they leave with a car trunkload of household belongings. Once the last child has left, the parents have few possessions to call their own.

Daughter number two came home from college last weekend. She arrived virtually emptyhanded, but she left with three plastic pails filled with cookies, one of my good blouses, and enough household furnishings to set up a small, second-hand store.

Before she returned to college, she walked through our house with the air of a prospective buyer. I remained close by her side as she quietly appraised the contents of the refrigerator and the bathroom shelves, my pots and pans and my household plants. Our house had become a flea market.

I nervously followed and watched as she looked through my jewelry box and held up one pair of earrings and then another. My earrings and other jewelry can hardly be compared with the crown jewels of England. In fact, they could be more accurately described as blue-light specials.

I tried to remain calm as she carefully examined our microwave oven. I would willingly bear arms in defense of that oven. In desperation, I reminded myself that her dormitory room was much too small and already too crowded to accomodate an appliance of that size.

We love our daughters dearly and we would gladly give them the shirts off our backs. My missing blouse attests to that fact.

Only one thing continues to puzzle me, however.

Why do they insist on lugging off our toaster, televisions, blankets, coffee pot and things that we still use? Why shouldn't they instead haul off their boxes of high school memorabilia?

Perhaps they assume, now that they have left for college, that those of us left at home have given up such mundane habits as eating and cooking.

By doing some tricky mental gymnastics, I have calculated that before our oldest two daughters graduate from college, we will be subjected to approximately 30 more weekend search-and-seizure operations.

By that time, and at the rate that things have been currently disappearing, we should be ready to move our meager collection of worldly goods into an efficiency apartment.

Homecoming

It's homecoming time. I'm not talking about that time of year when football teams do whatever they do on muddy fields, or when queens are crowned or when alumni come back and relive their golden years.

This kind of homecoming involves college students as they come home for the summer. It's the time of year when students consolidate the entire contents of their dormitory rooms and deposit said contents on the floors of their parents' kitchens, living rooms and hallways.

At this very moment, untold thousands of mothers across the country are washing mountains of clothing they haven't seen for two semesters. Normal passageways through houses are obstructed with boxes of term papers, textbooks and other items of unknown origin.

As surely as the swallows return to Capistrano, pillows, blankets, televisions and appliances, which we had never expected to see again, have returned to the roost.

Within two days' period of time, our two daughters returned from college and the result was having a home which resembled a warehouse for unclaimed freight. As any good mother would do in a similar situation, I took one look at the disarray, clutched my heart and went to bed with a headache.

I don't wish to leave the impression that our house is normally that immaculate. However, on a clear day one should be able to walk from the kitchen to the bathroom without breaking a leg or stumbling in the dark. Our kitchen was not designed to accommodate three toasters and enough clothing to take care of a third world country.

On the morning following the second daughter's homecoming, a miracle of sorts occured. The boxes mysteriously disappeared and our house appeared to be back to normal. It could have been condemned by *Better Homes and Gardens*, but it was normal. By some sleight of hand or some illusionary feat, our daughters had managed to squeeze what would have filled two train cars into two tiny closets upstairs.

I knew that if I would open one of those closet doors, it would be an invitation to certain death. I would succumb in a avalanche of sweaters, tennis shoes and half-empty bottles of shampoo. I would not be missed until the next mealtime.

Once I read about a reclusive, older woman whose body was found in a tiny apartment, which had been filled to the ceiling with old magazines, cardboard boxes filled with junk and other debris. She had been labeled as an eccentric collector.

After our recent invasion of cardboard boxes, I think that she should have been given the benefit of the doubt. She could have been the hapless victim of a daughter or son's college homecoming.

Parental Pride

It's definitely true. Pride goes before a fall.

Pride in one's children is like soaring the heavens with an inflated balloon. Once in a while, the balloon bursts.

Just ask my friend.

I know all about parental pride. When our children were very young, it didn't take much to make me proud. The days they stopped eating crayons and swallowing pennies were milestones in their lives. I dutifully recorded the dates of their first steps, first words and first days of school as though no other children in the world had ever done those things before.

When they were teenagers, immense moments of pride occured when they came home early from dates and went an entire year without school deficiencies. It didn't take much to have me talking enthusiastically about their successes.

I may not have invented parently pride, but I certainly honed it to a social art.

My friend was proud of her married daughter a short time ago. Her ecstasy lasted a full three minutes.

For Christmas, she and her husband gave their daughter and her husband a sum of money in lieu of some other gift. In the true spirit of the holidays, the young couple was told to spend it as they wished.

In other words, spend it sensibly. Make us proud. Buy something practical like underwear.

A few weeks later, my friend checked back with her daughter. After the usual pleasantries over the phone, she asked what they had done with the cash gift.

"Oh, we bought a CD," her daughter responded.

No parent has known a greater sense of pride than my friend knew at that exact moment.

A certificate of deposit! Accrued interest on the principle! These kids were sensible beyond their years. They were letting their money make more money. She and her husband must have been doing something right when they raised this wonderful, insightful daughter.

"Where did you buy the CD?" my friend asked her daughter, thinly disguising her swelling pride. She fully expected the answer to be the name of a bank or a savings and loan.

Instead, her daughter gave her the name of an audio store.

In one agonizing moment, my friend realized that her daughter would never become another Vanderbilt or Rockefeller.

Told to spend the money as they wished, the young couple purchased a compact disc player.

The Visit

They roamed from room to room in our house, taking everything in sight. As my husband and I stood dumbfounded in disbelief, they searched our house from attic to basement, leaving few things behind in their wake.

On of them spied some bookshelves in our basement.

"You don't really need these, do you?" she asked. She was the older of the two marauders.

"Not really", I answered weakly. After all, I reasoned, bookshelves can hardly be considered necessities in life, along with food, shelter and clothing. Bookshelves are not really basic to our existence.

"Good!" she replied amiably. "I'll carry them out to the car."

As you might have guessed by now, our college daughters came home for the weekend. We knew that they really wanted to see us this time, because most of our valuables have already been stashed away in their college dorm rooms. With our television, blankets, sheets and dishes already confiscated on previous pillaging missions, our property holdings have been reduced considerably.

During this past weekend, I realized that this visit gave them an opportunity to see if they had overlooked anything of value on previous trips.

Actually, it's fun to have the girls home for those all too brief weekends. It seems a real shame that when they can finally dress themselves and carry on intelligent conversations, they are sent off to remote colleges and we rarely get to see them. There's something wrong with the system.

Where were the colleges when we were feeding the girls strained carrots, starving their fevers, feeding their colds and fighting diaper rash? Where were those fine college advisors when the girls were going through their "terrible two's"?

It is downright considerate of those colleges to take care of them now, once they have become self-sufficient. Being a college is easier than being a parent.

It is not a fair trade-off. As parents we get to memorize all of Dr. Seuss's books while the colleges get to talk about medieval literature and foreign policy.

I also suspect that colleges subsidize their operating budgets by holding gigantic rummage sales every spring. Throughout the year they encourage their students to beg, borrow and steal their parents' lowly possessions and return them to the college after each visit home. That could account for the reason why we never see those objects again.

They will never get my microwave oven.

Chocolate for Cows

For most of my life, I have eaten for Third World countries. When I was young, my mother used to admonish me to clean my plate "because there are children starving in Asia and Africa."

I never could figure out how my cleaning my plate would ever put food on those other children's tables, but I was an obedient child. I finally rationalized that if my cleaning my plate would spare the rest of the world the experience of eating my mother's chili and other spicy delights, it was the least I could do. Ripping the chubby girl labels out of my dresses was a small price to pay for my mother's silence on the subject.

Our own daughters were considerably less obedient. When I threw them the line about starving children, their response was, "Well, send it to them." Needless to say, I landed up cleaning my plate as well as theirs. Old habits are hard to break.

Nothing I have ever wasted compares with what is going on right now in New Jersey, Maryland and Pennsylvania. Dairy farmers are feeding broken chocolate candy bars to their cows. Hershey Foods Corporation, in Hershey, PA, is selling damaged chocolate bars to farmers at the bargain shop price of $60 a ton. The chocolate is added to the rations of hay, soybeans, alfalfa and grains their herds consume.

The article I read in *The Wall Street Journal* went on to say that a candy bar has about twice the energy as an ear of corn. The chocolate is cheaper than corn, and the cows' butterfat content in their milk is up to 3.9 percent.

It's a disgrace. Haven't we done enough for dairy cows? I say we have. We've dedicated the entire month of June to milk products and we have dairy day festivals in many of our rural communities. Their lives weren't all that bad before they started eating chocolate. Otherwise, where would we have gotten the expression, "Contented as a cow?" Isn't it enough that we give them names like Nellie and Bossy and let them unload their burdens on us twice a day?

Personally, I have never objected to cows eating alfalfa, corn and soybeans, but when they start eating good chocolate, I believe that we must draw a line.

I could handle broken candy bars at $60 a ton. I could smash two halves together and pretend it was a whole bar. As far as I'm concerned, there are tons of broken chocolate somewhere in Pennsylvania with my name on them, and they are being shipped out to some pasture instead.

One farmer who was interviewed for the article noted, "If you put a pile of candy bars out in a pasture, the cows would eat themselves to death." It may sound disgusting, but I can identify with the bovines' passion for chocolate.

When it comes to this gross misuse of chocolate, I am truly convinced that cows are giving the rest of us a bum steer.

CAROLE ACHTERHOF is a long-time resident of Luverne, MN. She and her husband, Roger, are the parents of three daughters, Kristin, Linda and Marta.

In addition to teaching secondary Spanish and English, and serving as editor of the Okobojian, a weekly newspaper in Spirit Lake, IA, she is a weekly humor columnist for several newspapers in Iowa and Minnesota.

She attributes her drawing skills to a geology class taken at the University of Minnesota, Duluth, where she drew flowers in the margins of her class notes. Her professor refused to give her extra credit for her artistic efforts.

Free-lance artist JENNIFER FISHER found inspiration for the cover design by consuming and researching countless boxes of fine chocolates. A native of Grinnell, IA, Jennifer graduated from Macalester College, St. Paul, MN, in 1988.

Jennifer's future plans include the pursuit of a MSA degree in design. She currently lives in St. Paul.

Why not send additional copies of NEVER TRUST A SIZE THREE to those near and dear to you? It's a much better idea than cleaning the bathroom or stripping the kitchen floor wax.

For a mere pittance, $9.95, plus $2 for postage and handling, additional copies will be sent to your home.

Forward your orders to:

CAROLE ACHTERHOF
315 NORTH FREEMAN
LUVERNE, MN 56156

This order form may be photocopied.

Please send me _____ copies of NEVER TRUST A SIZE THREE at $9.95 plus $2 for postage and handling.

Enclosed is my check or money order for $_____, payable to CAROLE ACHTERHOF.

NAME _____

STREET_____

CITY_____STATE_____ZIP_____